TASTY
HIGH
PROTEIN

A total cracker of a dish!
My Chicken Pad Thai recipe
(page 110)

TASTY HIGH PROTEIN

Fraser Reynolds

TRANSFORM YOUR DIET

WITH EASY RECIPES

UNDER 600 CALORIES

EBURY
PRESS

CONTENTS

Hello!

Welcome! First of all, a massive thank you to everyone who has bought this book. For someone who started developing recipes in their mum's tiny kitchen, this is all a little surreal. I'm still pinching myself.

My aim was to show that tasty, high protein and nutritious meals need not cost the earth or take up too much of your valuable time. I love cooking and I wanted to share my creations, but never in a million years did I think it would come this far.

In the beginning, it was just me, a few pots and pans and some ideas in my mum's kitchen in Bannockburn, Scotland. My background had been co-owning and running a local CrossFit gym and managing a gym in Australia; before that I was a PE teacher, after graduating from the University of Stirling. Having done some kind of fitness training for most of my life, I had always been interested in nutrition. That interest developed and led to me gaining a variety of nutritional and gym-based qualifications, and I still love the educational side of fitness and food.

When I started creating the recipes, I was quite new to the concept of filming, editing and sharing them online. I had around 2,500 followers at the start, which was in May 2022. I wanted to show that cooking simple, nutritious and delicious meals could be done without too much fuss, and I knew that social media was the best place to do this if I wanted to reach a wider audience.

While I was training, I was always on the lookout for calorie-controlled, high protein and delicious food, and I couldn't see much of this online. The stuff that was there was a little complicated, included ingredients I could never find, or looked amazing but did not have the macronutrient content alongside the recipe. My plan was to show that, if meals could be made simply, I would be able to help a lot of people enjoy cooking while also helping them lose weight – if that was their aim.

I now have – amazingly – a social media following of over a million people. I can help a vast number of people eat more healthily and enjoy their food and – most importantly – we have a lot of fun while we're doing it. I try not to take myself too seriously, as anyone who follows my content will know. I still don't know what I was thinking with that hairstyle.

It feels pretty weird to write 'one million followers', considering how quickly it has all happened. I am beyond grateful for every like, share and comment that people have thrown my way.

One of the things I wanted to convey with my recipes was that eating a well-balanced diet does not have to be overly restrictive. In fact, it should be anything but. The key is in that all-important word, balanced.

I want to demonstrate, with easy-to-cook meals, that we can all have flexibility in our diet while at the same time smashing our health and well-being goals. A weekend away, a holiday, should not leave you feeling 'guilty' that you've fallen off the dietary wagon. That's not the way things have to be! Food is a beautiful thing, and we should all be able to enjoy it without worrying about the emotional baggage that we foist on ourselves.

Now, after coaching a variety of people for many years, each with their own fitness goals, I have gained a real appreciation of the importance of the right level of protein in our diet. While coaching my clients, a key part of helping people was developing a tailored dietary guide for them. On protein specifically, there is more detail below, but in my experience many of us are not eating enough of it. Neither are we always aware of the macronutrient content of the food we're consuming. And that's totally understandable, it's not an easy thing to monitor.

However, given that the food choices we make have a massive impact on achieving our goals – whether it's gaining strength, losing weight, or simply feeling a little better about ourselves – without the right nutrition, it is so much harder than it needs to be.

This book is your guide to changing that.

Before you get stuck in, please remember that these dishes are designed to be versatile and hopefully ignite that creative spark inside you!

Your encouragement means the world to me, and I always love your feedback. You can find me on all the usual social media channels.

Thank you all.

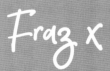

 @FraserReynolds   @Fraser__Reynolds   @fraser__reynolds

Why High Protein?

A quick word on why high protein meals are important.

Firstly, for weight loss. Protein is more satiating than carbohydrates and fats (these are the three macronutrients), which means that it can help you to feel full for longer throughout the day. This can be beneficial if you're running low on calories and want to avoid those moments of HANGER! Secondly, your body burns more calories breaking down protein than it does carbohydrates and fats, a process known as the thermic effect of food (TEF). The TEF is the energy your body needs to absorb and digest the food you eat. Protein has a higher thermic effect than carbohydrates and fats, so a high protein diet can actively support a calorie deficit if your goal is fat loss.

If your goal is fat loss, the underlying principle is that you must be in a calorie deficit. This means that you consume fewer calories than your body needs to maintain its current weight. You can achieve this either by reducing your calorie intake through diet or increasing your calorie expenditure through exercise or physical activity, or a combination of both. I recommend that my clients do both. Not only does this approach increase your ability to create a deficit, it also encourages you to maintain a healthy active lifestyle in the longer term. Exercise has huge benefits beyond physical health: it can boost your mood and for many it is a great tool for stress relief. Once exercise becomes part of our routine, we quickly realise that by improving one side of the equation it becomes easier to improve our habits on the other.

Protein can also improve muscle strength and function, so a high protein diet is key for those looking to build muscle. No, you're not going to turn into Arnold Schwarzenegger overnight, but protein is essential for the growth and repair of muscles. When we exercise – and especially during intense resistance-based forms of exercise – our muscle fibres are broken down and protein is essential for the support and repair of these fibres.

In addition, we tend to lose muscle mass and strength as we get older. Ensuring you have adequate protein in your diet can help support muscle function and mobility throughout your life.

SETTING YOUR NUTRITION TARGETS

People often ask me 'how much protein should I be aiming for per day?' The full answer is that it depends on your age, size, activity levels and whether you have any health concerns. Please bear in mind that I am not a medical practitioner, and you should seek qualified advice if you are in any doubt or if you have underlying medical conditions that could be impacted by a diet change.

But a good, rough rule of thumb is that you should aim for 0.8 to 1.2g of protein per 1lb of your ideal body weight. I say 'ideal' body weight because it makes this goal more realistic for most of us. If you currently weigh 240lbs and you're new to following a high protein diet, it's a big ask to be shooting for 240g per day. When setting your protein goal, I suggest keeping it realistic for you and your current lifestyle. Consistency is key, so start small and look to improve as your awareness of protein increases.

Before making your calculation it's important to consider your activity levels and the type of exercise you currently do. If your goal is building muscle or if you're following an intense exercise regime, I'd recommend aiming for the higher calculation of protein where possible; you'd also be looking at increasing your calorie intake. An example of an intense regime would be someone weightlifting or taking part in interval-style training for 30–60 minutes three or four times a week.

To work out your current total daily energy expenditure, learn more about macronutrients or establish what a calorie deficit would look like for you, I've created a free calorie calculator on my website. Please use the QR code above and fill in the details required. Health and fitness look different for everyone and it's so important to remember that there isn't a one-size-fits-all approach.

As a starting point, I would suggest that, once you've calculated your ideal daily calorie needs, you choose from one of the following two ratios and set this up on a food tracker (I use MyFitnessPal or Nutracheck). The ratios refer to the percentage of calories that come from each of the macronutrients (fat has twice the calories of protein or carbohydrates per gram). You're aiming for a 30% ratio of protein across the whole day: some meals will fall under or over that target.

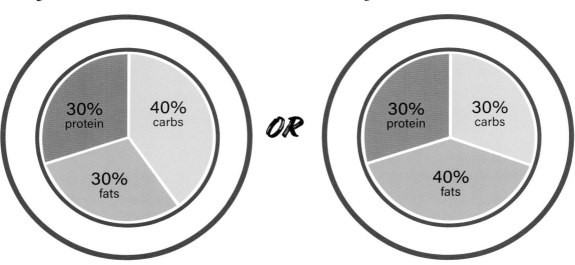

Higher carb ratio:

30% protein
40% carbs
30% fats

OR

Higher fat ratio:

30% protein
30% carbs
40% fats

If your goal is fat loss, either ratio will work. However, if you're following an intense exercise regime, you may wish to opt for a higher carbohydrate ratio. This is because during intense exercise your body uses glycogen as a fuel source to provide working muscles with energy. Carbs help to maintain glycogen levels and avoid fatigue, especially during exercise that requires short bursts of maximum effort.

How this book works

The book is structured into solutions-based chapters to help you find what you need throughout the week. There are recipes to suit all occasions. Some are perfect if you're cooking for yourself or for a couple, but all are easy to scale up, and I've created the recipes with a busy family in mind – so that you're not having to cook and eat separately.

All my recipes are high protein, with calorie and macronutrient information to help you reach your goals. Every recipe comes in at under 600 calories per serving – and that includes the sides!

I've included a barcode on every page that you can scan and use to log your meals into a food-tracking app (I use MyFitnessPal or Nutracheck).

BRUNCH

Delightful high protein breakfast options, including smoothies for a great start to any day of the week, chocolatey Overnight Oats, and Beans on Toast with a spicy twist. Or start your weekend off with a bang with Cottage Cheese Scrambled Eggs or a luxurious Smoked Salmon Hash. And how can you resist my gooey Baked Crumpets topped with raspberries and white chocolate?

QUICK BITES

As it sounds, guys. Throw these together in less than 30 minutes when you're short on time, but you still want to eat well. Alongside some high protein twists on sandwiches and wraps, get dinner on the table with coconutty Spicy Noodle Soup, Quick Flatbread Pizza or speedy Salmon Burgers.

FAMILY FAVOURITES

This is the category for the parents out there, with simple and straightforward meals that the kids will love. To keep things simple, all the recipes here serve 4. Nutritious and delicious, they keep the protein high and the calorie counts covered. Favourites old and new include a tasty Fish Pie, Hearty Veggie Chilli, Beef Stroganoff, Chicken and Chorizo Pie and Mac 'n' Cheese Bolognese.

FAKEAWAY

My take on some takeaway favourites. The taste you know and love, but in easy, affordable, calorie-controlled and high protein equivalents. If you go for Asian flavours, you'll love Chicken Pad Thai, Crispy Chilli Beef, Soya Chunk Kung Pao or a Prawn Massaman Curry; get messy with Dirty Fries or an Upside-Down Burger; not forgetting a healthier version of good old fish and chips.

AIR FRYER *and* SLOW COOKER

Who doesn't love one of these beauties? They really make life simple – just look at my Air Fryer Sticky Salmon and Air Fryer Doner Kebabs, or, from the slow cooker, Pulled Pork or aromatic Chilli Chicken Curry.

My air fryer has double rectangular drawers, 9.5-litre capacity and is 400 watts. If your air fryer is different, you may need to adjust cooking times slightly.

My slow cooker has a 5.6-litre capacity: you may need to adjust some recipes slightly if you have a smaller or larger slow cooker.

This book is designed to make each recipe easy and straightforward – we'll have you cheffin' in no time!

SIDES

This section gives loads of simple ideas for side dishes and accompaniments to suit every taste. Throughout the book I've suggested low calorie switches to give you options if you need a lower calorie meal: you'll find all the necessary information in this section. If you do swap the sides, remember to check this section to keep track of your calories and macros.

MEAL PREP

There's nothing better for the week than a fridge (or freezer) full of healthy options that take minutes to reheat. From my twist on a Gammon and Pea Soup to Creamy Cajun Chicken Pasta and a vegetarian Aubergine Moussaka, this chapter is your guide to high protein meal prep.

Some people have reservations about prepping meals in advance: they may think it will take too long or they don't know what they'll be doing in the week ahead. All I can say is, give it a bash, commit a jot of time over the weekend, and you will be amazed at the hours this gives you back throughout the week.

Planning out your week's meals and doing some cooking ahead of time is the approach I take when coaching my clients, and it's an ideal way to ensure that you don't have a midweek dietary stumble – although there's nothing wrong with enjoying yourself from time to time. But if you're keen to progress on the nutrition front, meal prepping is a game changer.

There are some things you need to consider for safe and successful meal prep:
- Always ensure your food has cooled before storing in the fridge or freezer: this usually takes around 90 minutes.
- Ensure your fridge is set to 2°C.
- Food can be stored in a covered container in the fridge for 2–3 days.
- The meals from this chapter can be frozen for up to 2 weeks.
- Defrost overnight in the fridge.
- When reheating, ensure food is piping hot throughout.

High Protein, Lower Calorie Swaps and Tips

Throughout the book you'll notice I mention lean, light and low in relation to ingredients. This is to highlight that when shopping, I opt for leaner mince, lighter cheeses and lower calorie alternatives where possible. Below I've given some details of the brands I've used when creating the recipes for this book, but if you're struggling with sourcing some of the ingredients, or you need to swap anything about, remember that a lean, light or lower calorie option will always be a better choice than the higher fat or higher calorie version. Here's a quick blast of some notable points.

MINCE

There's a lot of variation in the fat content of different types of mince. When it comes to beef, I always suggest 5% fat beef mince. If this is not available, I would opt for 10% fat and ensure you add the differences in nutritional value. For reference, 10% fat beef mince has 38 more calories, 4.9g more fat and 2g less protein per 100g. Both have 0g carbs.

Lamb: I always use 10% fat lamb mince.

Pork: I always use 5% fat pork mince but, if this is not available, I would opt for 10% fat and ensure you add the differences in nutritional value. For reference, 10% fat pork has 97 more calories, 10.8g more fat and 0.5g less protein per 100g. Both have 0g carbs.

CHEESE *and* OTHER DAIRY PRODUCTS

You'll see a whole array of lower fat alternatives around your supermarket. When it comes to cheese, as a general rule I opt for the 30% lighter versions as they taste the best and provide the lowest calories for the highest protein. In calculating the nutritional information for this book I've used light Cheddar with 22g fat per 100g. Light mozzarella has around 8g fat per 100g.

I use Philadelphia Light soft cheese, with 40% less fat (11g fat per 100g) than the original.

I use Flora light butter, with 28g fat per 100g.

I use 0% Fage Greek yoghurt, so look for fat-free Greek-style yoghurt.

VEGETARIAN *and* VEGAN OPTIONS

My go-to brands are Linda McCartney for sausages and high protein mince, Beyond Meat for burgers, and Tree of Life soya mince and soya chunks. The Tree of Life bad boys are only available in some of the big supermarkets but at a whopping 50% protein they can really help you hit your protein targets. Own-label soya mince and chunks often come in at 45–50% protein, so have a quick check of the label, but you can't go far wrong.

BREADS, WRAPS, BAGELS

In the Sides section I've included a variety of high protein and lower calorie options. Hovis Nimble Wholemeal bread has 50 calories per slice. Reduced calorie wraps, such as Deli Kitchen Carb Lite, will save you a good 50 calories per serve. Thin bagels are another great choice if you're on a calorie budget: Warburtons Protein Thin Bagels are packed with plant-based protein.

SWEETENERS

There's now a wide range of sugar alternatives made with stevia (which is extracted from a South American plant): these have no calories but can be used as a direct replacement for sugar. Pure Via and Truvia are widely available brands – I use Pure Via.

Some of my brunch recipes call for zero calorie syrup, and there are various brands and flavours available online and in shops and supermarkets but, if it's hard to find, you could use light agave nectar.

SHORTCUTS TO SAVE TIME *and* ADD FLAVOUR

Condensed soup is a little cheat code for the sauce in several recipes. Campbell's is my go-to brand.

Seasoning mixes, sauces and relishes are a great way of packing in the flavour. I have various jars of Schwartz seasonings, along with Old El Paso taco seasoning. For peri peri seasonings and sauces – Nando's! To add a touch of Thai flavour I use light sweet chilli sauce – Blue Dragon is widely available.

If you're in a bit of a hurry and need to save some time, I'm a big fan of Very Lazy Garlic (pre-cut garlic in a jar) and Very Lazy Ginger (some supermarkets have their own brands of ready chopped garlic and ginger). Another option is garlic or ginger paste (or purée): the work is already done for you, and you still get the same flavour contribution to your meal.

BRUNCH

Protein-Packed Smoothie Bowl 17

The Green Machine Smoothie 18

Cottage Cheese Scrambled Eggs 19

Creamy Eggs *on* Toast 20

Egg White Rolled Wrap 23

Onion, Mushroom *and* Cheese Frittata 24

Breakfast Muffin 25

Shakshuka 26

Breakfast Taco Wraps 28

Breakfast Pizza 30

Smoked Salmon Hash 33

Big Beans *on* Toast 34

Cookies *and* Cream Overnight Oats 36

Baked Protein Oats 38

Baked Crumpets 40

Fluffy Chocolate Protein Pancakes 42

PROTEIN-PACKED SMOOTHIE BOWL

You cannot beat a smoothie for something quick in the morning. Goes without saying that this is a great choice for making the night before, if you're going to be up and at it bright and early. This is a big favourite on social media, and it hits the spot with 39 grams of protein.

Like many of my recipes, this one has endless possibilities. Switch the yoghurt and protein powder flavourings, or change the frozen fruit to put your own spin on things.

250g frozen mixed berries
100g fat-free Greek-style yoghurt
1 scoop vanilla protein powder
1 tbsp chia seeds
1 tbsp shredded coconut

1. Put the frozen berries, yoghurt and protein powder into a blender and blitz until smooth.

2. Pour into a bowl and sprinkle with chia seeds and coconut.

TIP: If you prefer a thicker smoothie, try adding a couple of tablespoons of oats; or add a banana (ideally over-ripe) if you're looking for extra sweetness.

Serves 1 **Nutrition** | 395 calories | 39g protein | 36g carbs | 13g fat

The GREEN MACHINE SMOOTHIE

It's green, it's mean and it won't take more than 5 minutes. That last part doesn't complete the rhyme, but I'll be honest, I was struggling. This is really easy to make and can be done the night before. I've made this and taken it to the gym with me as a little post-workout refuel.

This is a healthy and nutritious start to your day, whacking in 28 grams of protein for only 259 calories, and is a good step on the way to your five a day. If you've got fresh spinach, add some ice for that ultimate frozen smoothie hit!

300ml unsweetened almond milk

100g frozen spinach

50g frozen berries

1 tbsp zero calorie syrup or light agave nectar

1 scoop vanilla protein powder

1. Pour all the ingredients into a blender and blitz for 45 seconds.

2. Pour into a large glass and enjoy.

TIP: If you fancy it, peanut butter will sweeten and add fibre to this smoothie. Just remember, it's 26 calories per 5g/teaspoon.

Serves 1

Nutrition | 259 calories | 28g protein | 26g carbs | 4g fat

COTTAGE CHEESE SCRAMBLED EGGS

A vegetarian dish that brings in the protein, with a considerable 33 grams. And with only 385 calories this is a great option if you're trying to lose weight. Or, depending on your viewpoint, it leaves you with lots of extra calories for the rest of the day, if you fancy a wee treat later on.

Changing the cheese is a nice way to play with this. Instead of Cheddar, some spicy cheese, for example, can add a little kick to this meal.

2 eggs
100g low-fat cottage cheese
1 tsp light butter
25g light Cheddar, grated
2 slices low calorie bread, toasted
salt and pepper

1. Beat the eggs in a bowl, season with salt and pepper, then stir in the cottage cheese.
2. Heat a pan over a medium heat. Add the butter and then the egg mixture and cook for 3–4 minutes, stirring continuously.
3. Add the grated cheese and mix well.
4. Serve on toasted bread.

CREAMY EGGS on TOAST

This vegetarian recipe is a delicious way to enjoy eggs for brunch. I would recommend it for all the family, and it's quick to make if you're in a rush. If you're cooking for someone who doesn't like spice, remove the sriracha and chilli flakes. If you love a little kick in your food, leave them in or even dial it up, depending on what floats your boat.

Experiment by varying the bread. I love my sourdough, and that works great here. Seeded bread is lovely too and helps with the protein count. Enjoy!

4 eggs
1 tbsp fat-free Greek-style yoghurt
1 tbsp light soft cheese
1 tsp paprika
4 tsp sriracha sauce
2 slices low calorie bread
handful of fresh chives, snipped
1 tsp chilli flakes (optional)
salt and pepper

1. Boil the eggs for 8–10 minutes: you want the yolks to be firm.
2. Drain the eggs and peel them. Cut them in half, adding the yolks to a bowl and setting the whites aside.
3. Add the yoghurt, soft cheese, paprika, sriracha, salt and pepper to the bowl with the yolks and mash to a creamy consistency. (You may need to add a splash of milk to help with this.)

4. Chop up the egg whites, then add to the mixture and mix well.
5. Toast two slices of bread and spread the mixture on top.
6. Add a sprinkle of chives and chilli flakes, if using, then serve immediately.

Serves 1

Nutrition | 419 calories | 32g protein | 24g carbs | 20g fat

EGG WHITE ROLLED WRAP

I discovered this one a few years back and it's a cracking start to any day. With 42 grams of protein for 394 calories, this ticks the protein box in a big way. My top tip for nailing this recipe is to ensure the egg whites are fully cooked before flipping. You can place a plate on top and flip the wrap out onto the plate, then slide it back into the pan if you're struggling with the flipping – I know I messed it up the first few tries! This might take you a few attempts to master but I can assure you it's worth it.

10–12 sprays light cooking oil
150ml egg whites
1 tsp paprika
1 tsp chilli flakes
1 low calorie wrap
2 tbsp tomato ketchup
2 slices turkey bacon, grilled
25g light Cheddar, grated
salt and pepper

1. Heat a frying pan over a medium heat and spray with oil.
2. Put the egg whites in a bowl, add the paprika and chilli flakes and season with salt and pepper.
3. Pour the mixture into the pan and heat for 1 minute.
4. Place the wrap on top and cook for a further 3 minutes.

5. Flip the wrap over, then add the ketchup, grilled turkey bacon and cheese.
6. Remove from the pan and roll up tightly. Cut in half and serve immediately.

Serves 1 | **Nutrition** | 394 calories | 42g protein | 27g carbs | 11g fat

ONION, MUSHROOM *and* CHEESE FRITTATA

A fabulous frittata is a staple of any brunch menu and couldn't be simpler to throw together – my kinda dish! This one is also ideal for meal prep: once sliced it should stay fresh in the fridge for 2–3 days. Eat it cold, heat it up or cover it in your favourite sauce. A cracking start to any day.

10–20 sprays light cooking oil
2 red onions, finely diced
200g mushrooms, sliced
2 tbsp smoked paprika
6 eggs, beaten
1 tbsp fresh chives, finely snipped
2 large tomatoes, diced
60g light Cheddar, grated
salt and pepper

1. Preheat the oven to 200°C/180°C fan/gas 6. Coat a tart tin with half the cooking oil spray.

2. Heat a pan over a medium heat and spray with the remaining oil. Add the onions and mushrooms, smoked paprika and plenty of black pepper and cook for 6–8 minutes until the onions are soft.

3. Add the veg to the tart tin, then add the eggs, chives, tomatoes and salt.

4. Sprinkle the cheese on top, then bake for 20 minutes or until a skewer comes out clean.

5. Leave to cool slightly before cutting into slices.

Serves 2 | **Nutrition** | 407 calories | 32g protein | 26g carbs | 22g fat

BREAKFAST MUFFIN

You really must try this – it's a belter! No getting in the car and sitting in a drive-through queue for you. Oh no, those days are done. Once you have the ingredients, your brunch experience will hit new heights in the comfort of your own home.

At 441 calories and 35 grams of protein, this meaty muffin is a top choice to start your day. Perfect for a Sunday morning late breakfast.

80g lean beef mince (5% fat)
1 tsp olive oil
10–20 sprays light cooking oil
1 egg
½ slice Red Leicester cheese
1 wholemeal muffin
1 tbsp light mayonnaise
1 tbsp tomato ketchup
salt and pepper

1. Combine the mince with the olive oil, salt and pepper, mix well and then form into a burger patty shape.

2. Heat a pan over a medium heat and spray with a little cooking oil. Add the patty and cook for 8–10 minutes.

3. Crack the egg into a cup. Put an egg ring (or a round biscuit cutter) into the pan and lightly spray with oil. Pop the egg into the egg ring and mix lightly.

4. While the egg is cooking, pop the cheese on top of the patty. Cover the pan to encourage the cheese to melt.

5. Split the muffin and toast in the toaster.

6. Mix the mayonnaise and tomato ketchup together, then spread over the insides of the muffin.

7. To serve, add the cooked patty and put the egg on top.

Serves 1

Nutrition | 441 calories | 35g protein | 29g carbs | 20g fat

SHAKSHUKA

Sounds fancy doesn't it? One of your workmates asks what you got up to over the weekend and you casually respond with 'Oh yeah, I made shakshuka'. As you do. This is a beautiful dish that provides 29 grams of protein and it's superb for a brunch, a lunch or whenever you fancy.

Cook the eggs to your preference, and serve with some crusty bread to help soak up the rest of it. This is a great one for meal prep: double up the ingredients for the spicy tomato mixture and reheat however much you want, adding the eggs and mozzarella for a really easy meal.

1 tbsp olive oil
1 onion, chopped
1 red pepper, chopped
3 garlic cloves, chopped or crushed
2 x 400g tins chopped tomatoes
1 tbsp smoked paprika
1 tbsp ground cumin
1 tbsp chilli flakes
fresh basil, roughly chopped
6 eggs
125g light mozzarella, sliced
3 slices crusty tiger bread
salt and pepper

1. Heat the olive oil in a large, deep frying pan. Add the onion, red pepper and garlic and fry until soft.
2. Add the tomatoes, smoked paprika, cumin, chilli flakes, salt and pepper, then sprinkle some basil into the mixture.
3. Cover the pan and simmer for 10 minutes.

4. Make six small hollows in the mixture and break an egg into each. Cover the pan and cook until the eggs are done in the way you like them.
5. Add the sliced mozzarella to the pan and sprinkle with pepper and more basil. Cover and cook until the cheese has melted.
6. Serve with crusty bread.

Serves 3 | **Nutrition** | 463 calories | 29g protein | 43g carbs | 19g fat

BREAKFAST TACO WRAPS

Is it a burrito. Is it a taco? I don't really know. What I do know is that these are cheesy and delicious, and there are so many possibilities to make them your own. You can change the seasoning, add your favourite sauce or add some chillies for that ultimate spicy kick.

It's also a really good choice for meal prepping in advance, then just whack in the oven for the ultimate crunch!

10–12 sprays light cooking oil
500g lean beef mince (5% fat)
1 onion, finely sliced
2 tbsp taco seasoning
   (I use Old El Paso)
50g jalapeños, diced (I use jarred)
2 garlic cloves, chopped
4 light cheese triangles
100ml boiling water
4 wraps
60g light Cheddar, grated
salt and pepper

1. Preheat the oven to 220°C/ 200°C fan/gas 7.
2. Heat a pan over a medium heat and lightly spray with oil. Add the beef mince and gently fry until it is no longer pink.
3. Add the onion, taco seasoning, jalapeños, garlic, salt and pepper and gently fry for 2–3 minutes.
4. Add the cheese triangles and boiling water and stir to create a creamy consistency.

5. To assemble, divide the mixture among the four wraps, add 15g of the grated cheese to each, then fold into burrito shapes and place in a baking dish. Cover with foil and bake for 6 minutes.
6. Cut in half and serve.

Serves 4 | **Nutrition** | 412 calories | 37g protein | 37g carbs | 12.5g fat

BREAKFAST PIZZA

This is one of my all-time favourite brunch meals, any day of the week. It always feels a bit wrong having a pizza for breakfast, the sort of thing I used to do as a student. But when it's only 406 calories with 37 grams of protein we can technically call it a healthy option, can't we? It's nice and quick to put together, and the cooking is easy as it simply goes in the oven.

I know it's a brunch dish the whole family will enjoy. Spice it to your taste with chilli flakes – I love chipotle chilli flakes for this.

10–12 sprays light cooking oil

1 low calorie wrap

2 eggs

100ml egg whites (enough to cover the wrap)

3 small tomatoes, chopped

handful of shredded spinach

1 tsp paprika

1 tsp chilli flakes

20g light Cheddar, grated

salt and pepper

1. Preheat the oven to 220°C/ 200°C fan/gas 7.

2. Spray an ovenproof pan with a little oil and add the wrap.

3. Crack the eggs onto the wrap and spoon in the egg whites to coat the remaining parts of the wrap.

4. Add the tomatoes and spinach, ensuring that you don't break the egg yolks.

5. Sprinkle with salt and pepper, paprika, chilli flakes and cheese, then bake for 8–10 minutes until the eggs are just set. Serve immediately.

Serves 1 | **Nutrition** | 406 calories | 37g protein | 24g carbs | 17g fat

SMOKED SALMON HASH

Smoked salmon – one of my favourite foods, regardless of what meal or time of day it is – takes this potato hash to a whole new level. It feels quite luxurious. Who would have thought that lime and mustard would go together so well? This is an absolute treat for a brunch, and not too heavy on the calories. It will keep you going for hours and hours.

1 tbsp olive oil

1 onion, finely diced

300g potatoes, peeled and cut into cubes

180g hot-smoked roasted salmon, flaked

juice of 1 lime

2 tbsp soured cream

1 tsp Dijon mustard

1 tbsp fresh parsley, finely chopped

2 tbsp fresh chives, snipped

1 tbsp mixed dried herbs

2 slices sourdough bread (100g)

1 lemon, cut into wedges

salt and pepper

1. Heat a frying pan over a medium heat, add the oil, then the onion and potatoes. Season with salt and pepper, then fry for 15 minutes, turning every few minutes, until the potatoes are cooked.

2. In a large bowl, combine the salmon, lime juice, soured cream, mustard, parsley and chives.

3. Once the potatoes are cooked, sprinkle over the mixed herbs and stir to coat, then add the salmon mixture. Turn off the heat and stir to coat the potatoes in the mixture.

4. Serve on a chunky slice of sourdough bread, with lemon wedges on the side.

Serves 2

Nutrition | 460 calories | 30g protein | 49g carbs | 18g fat

BIG BEANS on TOAST

The student classic. To be honest I still love beans on toast when I'm feeling lazy – absolutely hee-haw wrong with the quick choice. This time, however, we are going to elevate the classic with these big, bold and bossy beans! We're adding a grown-up twist to this dish – not something I am often accused of doing. If you're looking for a lower calorie option, switch out the sourdough and opt for some lower calorie bread.

Let's get cheffin'!

60g chorizo, diced
1 onion, diced
1 large red pepper, diced
2 garlic cloves, finely chopped
2 tbsp ground cumin
1 tbsp smoked paprika
1 tbsp chilli flakes
1 x 400g tin cannellini beans
200g butter beans
1 x 400g tin chopped tomatoes
50g light mozzarella, chopped
    into chunks
2 slices sourdough bread (100g),
    toasted

1. Heat a frying pan over a medium heat, then add the chorizo and cook for about 3 minutes, until crispy.
2. Add the onion, pepper and garlic and cook for a further 3 minutes.
3. Add the cumin, smoked paprika and chilli, stirring continuously.
4. After 1 minute add the beans and tomatoes. Cover the pan and simmer for 5 minutes over a low heat.

5. Meanwhile, preheat the grill to medium.
6. Sprinkle the cheese over the beans, then place under the grill for 3 minutes until the cheese has melted.
7. Serve on toasted sourdough bread.

Serves 2 | **Nutrition** | 510 calories | 34g protein | 53g carbs | 15.5g fat

COOKIES *and* CREAM OVERNIGHT OATS

Utter bliss. You'll be waking up with a big cheesy grin knowing this is waiting for you. It's a really simple recipe and I'm a fan of prepping a few of these in advance to demolish over the coming days. The kids will absolutely love this, and you'll have no difficulty in getting them to sit down to eat it. It could also be a great treat if you have people visiting. Remove the protein powder if you prefer.

50g rolled oats

120ml unsweetened almond milk

15g chocolate protein powder

4 tsp zero calorie syrup or light agave nectar

3 cookies and cream biscuits (I use Oreos)

80g fat-free Greek-style yoghurt

1 tbsp light soft cheese

2 tbsp cocoa powder

1. In a meal prep container, combine the oats, almond milk, protein powder and 3 teaspoons of the syrup; place in the fridge overnight.

2. The next day, pull the cookies apart and scrape the white centres into a bowl. Add the yoghurt, soft cheese, cocoa and the remaining 1 teaspoon of syrup and stir to mix. Spoon on top of the oat mixture.

3. Bash up the biscuit parts of the cookies to a rough crumb and sprinkle on top.

4. Serve immediately with your morning cuppa.

Serves 1

Nutrition | 453 calories | 31g protein | 56g carbs | 13g fat

BAKED PROTEIN OATS

Baked oats take a little longer to prepare than regular oats – but they're so worth the wait! This is super simple and once in the oven will give you plenty of time for a cuppa, the washing-up or running around after the kids.

The chocolate chips and marshmallows create a warm, gooey, chocolate yumminess. A real weekend indulgence that will have you dreaming of seconds.

1 tbsp peanut butter

20g rolled oats

20g vanilla protein powder

1 tsp ground cinnamon

½ tsp vanilla extract

50g fat-free Greek-style yoghurt

½ ripe banana

2 tbsp unsweetened almond milk

1 tbsp zero calorie syrup or light agave nectar

8–10 sprays light cooking oil

10 chocolate chips

10 mini marshmallows

1. Preheat the oven to 200°C/180°C fan/gas 6.

2. Put all the ingredients – except the cooking oil, chocolate chips and marshmallows – into a blender and blitz until smooth.

3. Lightly spray a baking dish with oil, then pour in the mixture.

4. Bake for 15–20 minutes. To test if it's done, insert a thin knife: it should come out clean.

5. Scatter the chocolate chips and marshmallows on top. Serve immediately.

TIP: For the ultimate indulgence, drizzle with low calorie choc fudge sauce (I use Sweet Freedom). Quality!

Serves 1 | **Nutrition** | 399 calories | 33g protein | 39g carbs | 12g fat

BAKED CRUMPETS

Hot, gooey and bursting with flavour. The perfect start to your day, with a whopping 30 grams of protein. To keep the calories low I've used egg whites; however, if you want to go all out, add the yolks too.

This breakfast is very versatile. I've tried lots of different fruits and sauces on top, so have some fun here. It's a great one to get the kids involved with, letting them pick the toppings. Ice cream? Sure, why not?

8–10 sprays light cooking oil

2 crumpets (I use Warburtons), cut into chunks

2 egg whites, whisked

50ml unsweetened almond milk

1 tsp ground cinnamon

20g vanilla protein powder

1 tsp zero calorie sweetener

5 raspberries, cut in half

15g white chocolate, melted

1 tsp icing sugar

1. Preheat the oven to 200°C/180°C fan/gas 6.

2. Spray a small baking dish with oil, then add the chopped-up crumpets.

3. Put the egg whites into a bowl and mix in the almond milk, cinnamon, protein powder and sweetener. Pour the egg white mixture over the crumpets and mix well.

4. Bake for 15 minutes until the mixture is just beginning to set.

5. Pop the raspberries on top, then drizzle over the melted white chocolate and finish with a light dusting of icing sugar.

Serves 1

Nutrition | 422 calories | 30g protein | 58g carbs | 7g fat

FLUFFY CHOCOLATE PROTEIN PANCAKES

Fluffy Chocolate Protein Pancakes. Now there are some words that go well together. It's got the sweet toothed people covered, it's got the kids covered, and it's got the people watching the calories covered as well, at 391 calories with 30 grams of protein. You can't lose with this one. It could be something that you serve as a special breakfast if you've got guests round, or make it a weekly treat for you and the family. Something for everyone to look forward to, and it could be your side of the deal for the kids finally cleaning their room.

Ensure you whisk the mixture well – you don't want any lumps. Fully preheat your pan to limit the stickiness.

1 x 200g pot chocolate protein pudding (available from Aldi and Lidl)
3 tbsp plain flour
½ tsp baking powder
1 tsp zero calorie sweetener
1 egg, beaten
8–10 sprays light cooking oil
6 strawberries
1 tsp chocolate fudge sauce (I use Sweet Freedom Choc Shot Fudge)
icing sugar, for dusting

1. Spoon the chocolate pudding into a large bowl and add the flour, baking powder, sweetener and egg. Whisk well until smooth.
2. Heat a frying pan over a medium-high heat, spray with a little oil, then spoon 1 tablespoon of the pancake mixture into the pan.

3. Cook for 2–3 minutes on each side until the edges begin to set. As you cook the pancakes, stack them up on a plate: you should have 3–4 pancakes. Top with strawberries, choc fudge sauce and a dusting of icing sugar.

Serves 1 (makes 3–4 pancakes)

Nutrition | 391 calories | 30g protein | 46g carbs | 9.3g fat

QUICK BITES

Spicy Noodle Soup 46

Julius Caesar Salad 49

Smoky Egg Bagel 51

Peri Peri Wrap 52

Easy Banh Mi 54

Quick Pizza Wrap 56

'Fish Finger' Sandwich 58

Coronation Chicken Sandwich 60

Salmon Burgers 61

Cheesy Turkey Burritos 62

Crispy Turkey Stir Fry 65

Quick Basil Beef Curry 66

Beefy Noods 68

Coconut Chicken Curry 70

Chicken Sausage Mac 'n' Cheese 71

Pistachio Crusted Salmon *with* Lemon Peas 72

SPICY NOODLE SOUP

I am always looking for ways to make new high protein soups, and this one is a belter! It's a twist on the popular laksa soup, with fewer calories. Extremely easy to make, this is definitely a top pick for the weekend's prep work. You can then take the soup to work with you and it's tasty whether it's hot or cold.

50g rice noodles
8–10 sprays light cooking oil
2 garlic cloves, finely chopped
340g raw king prawns, peeled and deveined
500ml boiling chicken stock
3 tbsp laksa paste
1 x 400ml tin light coconut milk
handful of beansprouts
2 tbsp fresh coriander, roughly chopped
1 red chilli, finely chopped

1. Place the rice noodles in a bowl of boiling water and leave them to soften.

2. Heat a pan over a medium heat and spray with cooking oil. Add the garlic and prawns and cook for 2 minutes.

3. Add the stock, laksa paste and coconut milk and bring to a simmer.

4. Add the beansprouts and bring back to the boil, then remove from the heat.

5. Drain the noodles and divide between two deep soup bowls. Ladle the soup on top and sprinkle with the fresh coriander and chilli.

Serves 2 | **Nutrition** | 377 calories | 28g protein | 32g carbs | 16g fat

JULIUS CAESAR SALAD

You see Caesar salad on every menu, but you might not necessarily think of it as a high protein choice. Well, that's all changed! This version includes chicken to boost the protein and is packed full of vitamins and minerals from the veggies.

We're looking at about 10–15 minutes for this meal, and that's including the prep work. A perfect option for your lunch. Working at home, this is the sort of thing I go for if I'm in a hurry.

80g romaine lettuce, torn into pieces
½ yellow pepper, sliced
½ carrot, peeled and shredded
100g baby tomatoes, halved
100g cooked chicken, sliced
Black pepper to garnish

Caesar dressing
80g fat-free Greek-style yoghurt
1 tsp olive oil
1 tbsp Worcestershire sauce
2 tbsp grated Parmesan
1 garlic clove, finely chopped
juice of ½ lemon
salt and pepper

1. To make the dressing, in a bowl combine the yoghurt, olive oil, Worcestershire sauce, Parmesan, garlic, lemon juice and salt and pepper to taste, and mix well.

2. Put the lettuce, pepper, carrot, tomatoes and chicken into a large bowl. Pour over the dressing and mix well.
3. Serve immediately, with plenty of freshly ground black pepper.

Serves 1 | **Nutrition** | 383 calories | 46g protein | 19g carbs | 14g fat

SMOKY EGG BAGEL

A bagel really is the classic way to start your day. It feels like a treat, but it's not too heavy on the calories and it's easy to put together. This packs in the protein and healthy fats. For a little extra reward, a slice of smoked salmon or a slice of spicy cheese is a beautiful addition, but bear in mind that this will add calories and change the macronutrient balance.

2 hard-boiled eggs, chilled, peeled and roughly chopped
25g light Cheddar, grated
2 tbsp red pepper, diced
2 tbsp red onion, very finely chopped
1 tbsp jalapeños, finely chopped
1 tbsp smoked paprika
1 tbsp fresh coriander, finely chopped
2 tbsp light mayonnaise
salt and pepper
1 thin bagel (I use Warburtons Protein Thins), split

1. Combine all the ingredients in a bowl and mix well.

2. Spread the mix over both halves of the bagel and serve immediately.

Serves 1 | **Nutrition** | 450 calories | 29g protein | 35g carbs | 21g fat

PERI PERI WRAP

A nice weekend treat. If you're cooking for a couple or a crowd, simply double up this recipe as required. It's also a great option for an office lunch or a post-workout snack.

Peri peri sauce is available in several flavours: any of them will be great with this dish.

150g frying steak, cut into strips
1 tbsp peri peri seasoning
1 tsp paprika
1 tsp garlic salt
10–12 sprays light cooking oil
¼ onion, finely diced
¼ red pepper, cut into strips
2 tbsp peri peri sauce
2 light cheese triangles
1 wrap
1 tbsp ready-made salsa

Low calorie switch:
low calorie wrap

1. In a small bowl, combine the steak with the peri peri seasoning, paprika and garlic salt.
2. Heat a frying pan over a medium heat and spray with cooking oil. Add the steak and cook for 2–3 minutes until browned all over, then remove from the pan and set to the side.

3. Reduce the heat under the pan, add the onion and pepper and cook until softened.
4. Add the peri peri sauce and the cheese and stir well.
5. Put the steak back in the pan and cook until the sauce thickens.
6. Warm your wrap, then spread the salsa across it.
7. Add the steak, roll it up and enjoy.

Serves 1 | **Nutrition** | 473 calories | 46g protein | 30g carbs | 18g fat

EASY BANH MI

If you've ever been to Southeast Asia you'll know that these filled baguettes are a staple. During my time in Vietnam I would visit the same family-run *banh mi* stand almost every day for a little chit-chat.

These make a change from your usual sandwich for work, although be prepared for your colleagues asking where you 'bought' them! If you like an extra kick, you can add some sriracha sauce.

1 tbsp honey
1 tbsp light soy sauce
1 tbsp hoisin sauce
1½ tbsp sesame oil
2 garlic cloves, finely chopped
300g skinless chicken breast,
  chopped into chunks
10–12 sprays light cooking oil
2 baguettes
3 tbsp light mayonnaise
1 tbsp liquid seasoning (I use Maggi)
½ cucumber, cut into ribbons
2 handfuls of fresh coriander
2 green chillies, sliced

Quick pickled carrot
2 tbsp zero calorie white sweetener
1 tbsp rice vinegar
1 tbsp salt
250ml hot water
1 carrot, peeled and cut into
  matchsticks

Low calorie switch:
low calorie wrap

1. First, make the pickled carrot: combine the sweetener, vinegar, salt and hot water in a bowl and stir to dissolve, then add the carrot and set aside.
2. In another bowl, mix the honey, soy sauce, hoisin sauce, sesame oil and garlic. Add the chicken and leave in the fridge to marinate for 15 minutes.
3. Heat a pan over a medium heat and spray with cooking oil, then fry the chicken for 10–12 minutes until fully cooked through.

4. Drain the pickled carrot.
5. Slice the baguettes in half lengthways. Spread the mayonnaise on both halves of the baguettes, then add the liquid seasoning.
6. Add the cooked chicken to the baguettes, followed by the pickled carrot, cucumber, coriander and chillies. Serve immediately.

Serves 2 | **Nutrition** | 543 calories | 45g protein | 59g carbs | 15g fat

QUICK PIZZA WRAP

We all love the idea of home-made pizza, but it sounds like something that's going to take a lot of work, doesn't it? Well, not with this cheeky wee number! Now you can whip up your own 'pizza' in less than 15 minutes. Happy days, eh?

You can have some fun with this one, adding other vegetables or sauces for a change. If you're serving this one to kids you might want to swap the wrap for a flatbread so that the base is a bit sturdier. Just remember to update the calories if you're tracking your meals.

1 high protein wrap or flatbread (I use Deli Kitchen Carb Lite Wraps)
1 tbsp pizza sauce
1 tsp dried oregano
½ red onion, sliced
¼ red pepper, sliced
6 jalapeños, sliced
100g cooked chicken, shredded
30g light Cheddar, grated

1. Preheat the oven to 200°C/180°C fan/gas 6.
2. Put the wrap or flatbread on a baking sheet. Spread the pizza sauce over, then sprinkle over the oregano.

3. Add the onion, pepper, jalapeños, chicken and cheese.
4. Place in the oven for 6 minutes until the cheese has melted. Serve immediately.

TIP: You can also grill this pizza! Just make sure you preheat the grill and keep an eye on it as you go!

Serves 1 | **Nutrition** | 415 calories | 38g protein | 45g carbs | 8g fat

'FISH FINGER' SANDWICH

When I was a student, I used to live off these. I still love them from time to time, although I doubt the ones I ate back then were as healthy as this version.

There are quite a few ingredients, so do ensure that they're all on the shopping list. The cheese – perhaps a surprise ingredient – works really well: I know you'll love it! This recipe is also a great way to get some healthier food into your little ones, as chances are they already like fish fingers.

2 tbsp plain flour

1 tsp turmeric

1 tsp chilli powder

1 tsp garam masala

4 tbsp egg whites

50g panko breadcrumbs

2 skinless white fish fillets, about 150g each

2 tbsp light mayonnaise

2 tbsp fat-free Greek-style yoghurt

4 pickles, finely diced

1 tbsp fresh parsley, finely chopped

1 tbsp fresh dill, finely snipped

1 tsp onion granules

4 slices low calorie bread

2 handfuls of shredded lettuce

2 cheese slices

salt and pepper

1. Preheat the oven to 220°C/200°C fan/gas 7. Line a baking tray with greaseproof paper.

2. Put the flour on a dinner plate, add the turmeric, chilli powder and garam masala and mix well.

3. Put the egg whites in a small bowl and put the breadcrumbs on another dinner plate.

4. Coat each piece of fish in the flour and shake off any excess.

5. Dip the fish into the egg whites, allowing any excess egg to drip back into the bowl.

6. Next, coat the fish in the breadcrumbs, pressing down firmly. Put the fish on the lined tray and bake for 12–14 minutes, carefully turning after about 7 minutes, or until golden brown.

7. Meanwhile, in a small bowl combine the mayonnaise, yoghurt, pickles, parsley, dill, onion granules and salt and pepper. Spread this over all four slices of bread. Top with the shredded lettuce.

8. Once the fish is cooked, put a slice of cheese on top of each fillet and return to the oven until the cheese melts.

9. Remove from the oven and place on two slices of bread. Cover with the other slices of bread, cut in half and serve.

Serves 2 | **Nutrition** | 490 calories | 44g protein | 51g carbs | 11g fat

CORONATION CHICKEN SANDWICH

Who doesn't love a bit of coronation chicken in a sandwich? Once you've tasted this, you know you'll make it again and again. It takes around 10 minutes all-in, so this really is the go-to option if you're in a hurry. The kids will love it too.

For a bit of variety, swap the bread. Sourdough is always a winner, or some high protein seeded bread works well in a sandwich.

125g cooked chicken, shredded

2 tbsp light mayonnaise

1 tbsp curry powder

1 tbsp mango chutney

1 tsp sultanas

1 tsp flaked almonds

salt and pepper

2 slices low calorie bread

100g crunchy salad (see Sides, page 209)

1. Combine all the ingredients in a bowl, then spread onto the bread.

2. Serve with a crunchy salad.

TIP: If you want a change from sliced bread, then pop the mixture on top of a baked potato or into a pitta bread.

Serves 1 | **Nutrition** | 442 calories | 37g protein | 42g carbs | 14g fat

SALMON BURGERS

Fish on a burger? It's a bit unusual, but my goodness it works well! As a treat, I like this served with some sweet potato fries, but it's also great with a side salad and the whole family will love it. It's quick to throw together, perfect for the family evening meal – or keep some of the mixture in the fridge to cook later in the week.

400g cooked salmon
100g panko breadcrumbs
1 onion, finely diced
1 tbsp freshly chopped dill
1 egg, beaten
80g light mayonnaise
1 tbsp Dijon mustard
juice of ½ lemon
10–12 sprays light cooking oil
4 lower calorie burger buns, toasted
1 head of lettuce, shredded

Low calorie switch:
sandwich thin or thin bagel

1. Put all the ingredients – except the cooking oil, buns and lettuce – in a large bowl and mix with your hands until all the ingredients are combined.
2. Form into four burger-shaped patties.

3. Heat a frying pan over a medium heat and spray with cooking oil. Add the patties and cook for 4 minutes on each side until golden brown.
4. Place each patty on a toasted bun and top with the shredded lettuce and your favourite sauce.

Serves 4 | **Nutrition** | 468 calories | 30g protein | 48g carbs | 18g fat

CHEESY TURKEY BURRITOS

This will do for lunch, for dinner, and for anything in between. Could even eat it cold at the weekend, or cook it in advance for a picnic. And no matter when you eat it, it's packing 48 grams of protein per serving.

It's also a good snack for the kids: you can slice your burrito into smaller portions and share it out. Happy kids = happy parents.

10–20 sprays light cooking oil
1 red onion, finely chopped
2 garlic cloves, crushed
500g turkey mince (2% fat)
2 tbsp peri peri seasoning
1 red chilli, finely chopped
1 red pepper, finely diced
1 x 400g tin refried beans
2 tbsp ready-made salsa
90g light Cheddar, grated
4 large wraps
salt and pepper

Low calorie switch:
low calorie wrap

1. Heat a pan over a medium heat and lightly spray with cooking oil, then add the onion and cook until softened.
2. Add the garlic and turkey mince, then the peri peri seasoning, chilli and red pepper and cook for 8 minutes.
3. Stir in the refried beans, salsa and grated cheese and mix well. Cook for a further 3 minutes.

4. Warm the wraps.
5. Add the turkey mince mixture to the centre of the wraps, then fold into burrito shapes.
6. Spray a frying pan with a little cooking oil and fry the burritos for 3–4 minutes or until golden brown and crispy.

Serves 4 | **Nutrition** | 475 calories | 48g protein | 46g carbs | 10g fat

CRISPY TURKEY STIR FRY

With just a wee bit of chopping, crushing and grating you can throw this cracker together in 15 minutes – you can even cut out the crushing if you have a jar of ready chopped garlic.

Turkey mince is a brilliant choice of protein: it provides this dish with a massive 43 grams of protein per serving and it helps keep the calories down. For a vegetarian version, substitute your favourite high protein meat-free mince.

We normally would associate rice with a stir fry dish, but trust me, orzo works well. It has a little bit more substance that goes great with extra veg.

2 tbsp sesame oil
500g turkey mince (2% fat)
3cm fresh root ginger, peeled and grated
1 large garlic clove, crushed
4 spring onions, finely chopped
2 tbsp honey
2 tbsp light soy sauce
1 tbsp sriracha sauce
300g orzo
500ml boiling water
juice of 1 lime
handful of fresh coriander, roughly chopped

1. Heat 1 tablespoon of the sesame oil in a large frying pan over a medium-high heat.
2. When the oil is hot, add the turkey mince and break it up with a wooden spoon or spatula. Fry for 10–12 minutes until golden brown and crispy.
3. Add the ginger, garlic and spring onions to the pan and fry for another minute.
4. Stir in the honey, soy sauce and sriracha, then cook for a further 2 minutes.

5. In a separate pan over a medium heat, add the remaining tablespoon of sesame oil and then the orzo and gently fry for 1 minute.
6. Pour in the boiling water and leave the orzo to simmer for 14 minutes or until al dente.
7. Drain the orzo and mix with the lime juice.
8. Serve the orzo on four plates and spoon the turkey mince mixture on top, with a garnish of chopped coriander.

Serves 4 | **Nutrition** | 498 calories | 43g protein | 70g carbs | 5g fat

QUICK BASIL BEEF CURRY

A dream come true: a low calorie, high protein, authentic-tasting curry that's quick and easy to make. What's not to love? If you're eating this at work, your colleagues will be over in a flash, wanting to know where you got it and how much it cost: they're in for a surprise. Alternatively, this is a great option for the whole family. The kids might – *might* – even think about doing some chores in return for you cooking this again. But no guarantees, we're not miracle workers.

400g frying steak, cut into slices
1 tsp paprika
1 tsp dried oregano
2 tsp chilli flakes
1 tbsp olive oil
250ml skimmed milk
100g light soft cheese
50g Parmesan, grated
handful of basil
salt and pepper
2 packets microwave basmati rice
   (500g cooked weight)

1. Put the beef slices into a large bowl and combine with the paprika, oregano and 1 teaspoon of the chilli flakes. Season with salt and pepper, then pour in the olive oil and mix well.

2. Heat a frying pan over a high heat until very hot. Add the steak and stir-fry for 2–3 minutes.

3. In a bullet or blender combine the milk, soft cheese, Parmesan, the remaining chilli flakes and the basil. Blitz the mixture and pour over the cooked steak.

4. Serve immediately, with some basmati rice.

Serves 4

Nutrition | 469 calories | 34g protein | 40g carbs | 19g fat

BEEFY NOODS

This delicious beef recipe needs just a little chopping and frying to produce a super tasty meal that dishes up a whacking 44 grams of protein per serving.

If you want to be super organised, you could mix the marinade and sauce and pop them in the fridge on the night before you cook the meal. This way, when you come in from work, all you have to do is to throw it all together, giving you a really easy midweek treat. This will give you back some time and ensure you're hitting your macro targets – a win-win.

2 packets cooked udon noodles (600g)
600g flat iron steak, thinly sliced
5–6 sprays light cooking oil
1 onion, finely chopped
1 red or green pepper, diced
3cm fresh root ginger, peeled and finely chopped
2 bird's eye chillies, finely chopped
5–6 spring onions, sliced

Marinade

1 tbsp olive oil
½ tsp baking powder
1 tbsp cornflour
4 tbsp dark soy sauce

Sauce

3 tbsp zero calorie brown sugar alternative (I use Pure Via)
3 tbsp dark soy sauce
3 tbsp light soy sauce
1 tbsp chilli powder

1. Place the udon noodles in a bowl of cold water.
2. To make the marinade, combine all the ingredients in a bowl and stir well.
3. Place the sliced steak in the marinade, stir to coat, then set aside for 10 minutes.
4. To make the sauce, mix all the ingredients in a bowl.
5. Heat a pan over a medium heat and lightly spray with cooking oil. Add the steak and fry for 3–4 minutes until browned, then remove from the pan and set aside.

6. Into the same pan add the onion, pepper, ginger and chillies and cook over a medium heat for 5–6 minutes.
7. Drain the noodles.
8. Add the sauce and noodles to the pan, then add the steak and mix well.
9. Serve immediately, topped with the sliced spring onions.

Serves 4 | **Nutrition** | 535 calories | 44g protein | 51g carbs | 16g fat

COCONUT CHICKEN CURRY

Oh ya dancer – this is a taste sensation and so easy and quick to rustle up you will impress yourself, never mind your guests. It's very adaptable, so if you prefer a spicier dish you can add some chillies, but I love the creaminess of the coconut milk.

For additional midweek time-saving you could prepare the paste and cook the chicken up to step 3, set aside to cool, then leave in the fridge overnight. Then you have something to look forward to after a hard day at work – all you'll need to do is bring it to the boil and add the veg.

Healthy, delicious and packing 44 grams of protein in every serving – success in a bowl. To complete this meal I would serve it with jasmine rice.

10–12 sprays light cooking oil
600g chicken, cut into strips
2 tbsp curry powder
300ml boiling chicken stock
100g sugar snap peas, halved
  lengthways
100g baby corn, sliced diagonally
1 large red pepper, sliced
200ml light coconut milk
1 tbsp light soy sauce
juice of 1 lime
2 packets microwave jasmine rice
  (500g cooked weight)

Curry paste
30g pack of fresh coriander
1 red chilli, seeded
6 spring onions, roughly chopped
3cm fresh root ginger, peeled and
  grated
2 garlic cloves, peeled
grated zest of 1 lime

1. Start by making the curry paste. Blitz the coriander, chilli, spring onions, ginger, garlic and the lime zest in a food processor. Set aside.
2. Heat a pan over a medium heat and spray with cooking oil. Add the chicken and curry powder and cook for 6–7 minutes until browned.
3. Add the curry paste and cook for a further 1–2 minutes, then pour in the stock and bring it to the boil.
4. Turn the heat down to a simmer, then add the vegetables. Simmer gently for 4–6 minutes.
5. Stir in the coconut milk, soy sauce and lime juice. Serve immediately, with jasmine rice.

Serves 4 | **Nutrition** | 496 calories | 44g protein | 54g carbs | 11g fat

CHICKEN SAUSAGE MAC 'N' CHEESE

I should have called this one rapid mac 'n' cheese. Chicken sausages are a real time-saver and this recipe makes four servings, which means it's a go-to for advance meal prep. As you'd expect with that chicken sausage added in, this can help you smash your protein goal, with 35 grams per serving.

When making the sauce, give it your constant attention to ensure no lumps are forming.

10 chicken sausages
180g macaroni
20g light salted butter
30g plain flour
400ml semi-skimmed milk
1 tsp onion salt
handful of fresh parsley, chopped
1 tbsp chargrilled chicken seasoning (I use Schwartz)
70g light Cheddar, grated
30g Parmesan, grated

1. Preheat the grill to medium and pop the chicken sausages under the grill for 10–12 minutes until cooked through.
2. Meanwhile, bring a large pan of salted water to the boil and put the macaroni in to cook.
3. In another pan, melt the butter. Stir in the flour until smooth, then gradually add the milk, stirring constantly to prevent lumps from forming.

4. Add the onion salt, parsley, chicken seasoning and grated Cheddar and stir well.
5. Chop the cooked sausages into bite-sized chunks and add to the sauce mixture.
6. When the macaroni is cooked, drain and add to the sauce.
7. Serve immediately, sprinkled with Parmesan.

Serves 4 | **Nutrition** | 434 calories | 35g protein | 48g carbs | 11g fat

PISTACHIO CRUSTED SALMON with LEMON PEAS

This meal has a sort of first-date vibe about it. It's the sort of thing you would casually pull out of the bag if you were trying to impress someone. 'Oh yeah, no big deal, I just threw it together.' And the best part is, it's not even that difficult to make. Even though it may be a meal to impress, it has a good balance of macronutrients, and packs a substantial amount of protein within the calorie budget.

Instead of the mash you could serve this with your choice of rice, although it's sticky rice that gets my vote.

500g piece of salmon, skin removed
juice of 1 lemon
3 tbsp Dijon mustard
3 tbsp honey
1 tbsp fresh rosemary, finely
    chopped
80g pistachios, finely chopped
salt and pepper
600g mashed potatoes (see Sides,
    page 210)
1 lemon, cut into wedges

Lemon peas

1 tbsp olive oil
1 tbsp light salted butter
500g frozen peas
2 garlic cloves, peeled
grated zest of ½ lemon

Low calorie switch:
crunchy salad

1. Preheat the oven to 220°C/200°C fan/gas 7. Line a baking tray with greaseproof paper.
2. Place the salmon on the greaseproof paper and sprinkle generously with salt, pepper and lemon juice.
3. In a small bowl, combine the mustard, honey and rosemary. Mix well, then brush over the salmon, ensuring all areas are covered.
4. Scatter the pistachios on top, then bake for 14 minutes or until the salmon flakes when lightly touched with a knife.

5. Meanwhile, make the lemon peas: heat a pan over a medium heat, add the olive oil and butter and heat for 2 minutes. Add the frozen peas and garlic and cook for a further 2 minutes.
6. Grate the lemon zest over the top and season with salt and pepper. Remove the garlic cloves before serving.
7. Once the salmon is fully cooked, cut into four equal chunks and serve with the peas and mashed potatoes, with lemon wedges on the side.

Serves 4 | **Nutrition** | 599 calories | 40g protein | 56g carbs | 22g fat

FAMILY FAVOURITES

SCOTTISH CULLEN SKINK

If you live outwith (that's a proper word up here) Scotland, you might be wondering what on earth 'Cullen Skink' is. Prepare for your wee world to be rocked. It's one of our most famous dishes, and it's generally classed as a hearty soup. The protein comes from the haddock, or sometimes other fish – salmon works well. There are plenty of vegetables in the mix as well.

If you're looking to lower your calorie intake while hitting your protein goals, this excels on both counts. Get stuck in!

- 1 tbsp light unsalted butter
- 1 onion, finely diced
- 400g potatoes, peeled and cut into cubes
- 400ml boiling water
- 500ml semi-skimmed milk
- 1 bay leaf
- 3 smoked haddock fillets, about 500g total weight
- ½ small bunch of parsley, finely chopped
- 8–10 chives, finely snipped
- salt and pepper
- 4 slices crusty bread

1. Melt the butter in a large pan over a medium heat. Add the onion and gently cook until softened.

2. Add the potatoes and fry for a few minutes, then add the boiling water and simmer for 15 minutes.

3. In another pan add the milk, bay leaf and haddock. Bring just to a simmer and gently heat for 5 minutes.

4. Lift the haddock out of the milk and leave to cool for a few minutes before flaking into pieces.

5. Remove the bay leaf and return the haddock to the milk.

6. Pour the haddock and milk into the pan with the potatoes.

7. Add the parsley, chives, salt and pepper, then serve immediately, with crusty bread.

Serves 4

Nutrition | 402 calories | 34g protein | 45g carbs | 9g fat

CHICKEN *and* RICE SOUP

Super versatile, soups are fantastic as a lunch and I find this one to be super filling. It's full of vegetables, to help you hit your five a day, and is particularly good for lunch at work on those cold winter days.

You might want to double the ingredients of this recipe and make eight portions. Soup freezes well, so it's great to stock up.

2 large skinless chicken breasts
1 litre chicken stock
200g white rice
2 leeks, sliced
5–6 carrots, peeled and grated or diced
3 bay leaves
500–800ml vegetable stock
salt and pepper
4 slices crusty white bread

1. Put the chicken and stock in a pan and bring to the boil, then reduce the heat and simmer for 10–12 minutes until the chicken is cooked through.
2. In another pan, boil the rice until half cooked, then drain.
3. Remove the cooked chicken from the stock and shred, using two forks, then add back into the stock.

4. Add the leeks, carrots, rice and bay leaves to the chicken stock.
5. Add about 500ml vegetable stock and bring back to the boil. Reduce the heat, cover the pan and simmer until the vegetables and rice are fully cooked. You may want to add a little more vegetable stock.
6. Remove the bay leaves. Season the soup to taste with salt and pepper. Serve with crusty bread.

Serves 4

Nutrition | 436 calories | 28g protein | 75g carbs | 3g fat

TERIYAKI TOFU

A vegan dish that is packed with protein, using that most versatile of options, tofu. For this one, and most of my tofu recipes, I'm going for the extra firm variety. The softer stuff is great for soups and the Vietnamese noodle dish, *pho*, but I like a bit of crunch, and letting the tofu fry without moving it around will really help it to crisp up. Pressing the tofu to squeeze out excess water will also help it to go crispy.

Teriyaki sauce – any kind will be fine, but check the label to ensure it's vegan – is bouncing with flavour, and kids will love it. I'd also have this down as a meal you'd serve to impress, and it's easy to halve the quantities to make dinner for two.

800g extra firm tofu

2 tsp sesame oil

1 tsp salt

2 tsp ground ginger

2 tsp garlic powder

2 tsp zero calorie brown sugar alternative (I use Pure Via)

8 tbsp teriyaki sauce (I use Blue Dragon), or more to taste

2 tbsp sesame seeds to garnish

2 packets microwave jasmine rice (500g cooked weight)

Low calorie switch:
konjac rice or cauliflower rice

1. Start 24 hours in advance by pressing the tofu to remove excess water. To do this, wrap the tofu in a clean tea towel or a doubled sheet of kitchen paper, place a plate on top and weigh down with a tin of tomatoes or beans. Leave in the fridge overnight.

2. The next day, cut the pressed tofu into cubes.

3. Heat a large frying pan or wok over a medium heat, add the sesame oil and the tofu – you might need to cook the tofu in two batches. Add the salt, ginger, garlic powder and brown sugar, then leave the tofu to cook for about 4 minutes before carefully turning it over.

4. Cook each side in the same way, as far as you can: they don't all have to be exactly the same.

5. Once the tofu is cooked, drizzle the teriyaki sauce over it until fully coated.

6. Sprinkle with sesame seeds and serve with jasmine rice.

Serves 4 | **Nutrition** | 580 calories | 33g protein | 58g carbs | 24g fat

CHEESEBURGER PASTA

I have been making this for years. I'll have it for lunch, dinner or, I'll be honest, it even does the job as a little midnight snack from the fridge.

Condensed soup works excellently as the base for a sauce and really adds some flavour to this recipe. You can use more or less any type of pasta or grated cheese. For a vegetarian version, use meat-free mince and vegetable stock cubes.

10–12 sprays light cooking oil

1 onion, chopped

500g lean beef mince (5% fat)

1 tsp onion salt

2 tbsp plain flour

1 tin condensed tomato soup

2 beef stock cubes

240g rigatoni pasta

80g spicy mix cheese, grated

2 tbsp burger relish (I use Gourmet Burger Kitchen)

400g mixed leafy salad (see Sides, page 209)

1. Heat a pan over a medium heat and spray with cooking oil. Add the onion and gently fry for 4–5 minutes.

2. Add the mince and cook until browned.

3. Add the onion salt and flour, then the tomato soup.

4. Fill the soup tin with water and add this to the pan, then crumble in the stock cubes.

5. Add the pasta, bring to a simmer and cook until the pasta is al dente. You may need to add a little more hot water, though the idea is to create a thick sauce.

6. Stir in the cheese and burger relish, then serve immediately, with a leafy salad.

Serves 4 | **Nutrition** | 568 calories | 41g protein | 69g carbs | 14g fat

TURKEY MEATBALL SPAGHETTI

You'll be surprised at how easy it is to make the meatballs for this one, and they turn out fantastically well. The wine in the sauce is also a bit of a game changer, so if possible don't miss it out: the alcohol evaporates off as it boils, but it adds great flavour.

These meatballs work well with any number of recipes. If you're looking for a tasty snack for the workplace, or a main meal with some vegetables, they will do the job perfectly. Here, with some home-made sauce and spaghetti, you've made yourself a classic.

500g turkey mince (2% fat)
1 egg, beaten
70g fresh breadcrumbs
1 tbsp olive oil
260g spaghetti
1 tbsp light butter
1 onion, finely diced
5 garlic cloves, crushed
200ml red wine
2 x 400g tins chopped tomatoes
1 tbsp dried oregano
handful of basil, roughly chopped
salt and pepper

Low calorie switch:
courgette spaghetti (see Sides, page 209)

1. Preheat the oven to 220°C/200°C fan/gas 7.
2. In a large bowl, combine the mince, egg, breadcrumbs, olive oil, salt and pepper. Use your hands to make 16 similar-sized meatballs.
3. Place on a baking tray and bake for 14 minutes. Alternatively, air-fry at 200°C for 12 minutes, turning every 4 minutes to ensure they're evenly cooked.
4. Bring a large pan of salted water to the boil and put the spaghetti in to cook until al dente.

5. Heat a pan over a medium heat, add the butter, then add the onion and garlic and cook for 3–4 minutes until beginning to soften.
6. Add the red wine and simmer to reduce for 3 minutes.
7. Stir in the chopped tomatoes, oregano and basil.
8. Once the meatballs are fully cooked through, add them to the sauce mixture and mix well.
9. Drain the spaghetti and serve with the meatballs and sauce.

Serves 4 | **Nutrition** | 592 calories | 41g protein | 73g carbs | 11g fat

TIP: Use an
ice-cream scoop
and roll between
your hands to make
the ball shape.

MAC 'N' CHEESE BOLOGNESE

This is my twist on a classic. Something I often hear from parents cooking for their little ones is that it can be difficult to get them to eat meat. In this dish that lovely protein source is hiding under one of the all-time kids' favourites. I'm a huge fan of dishes like this that allow the whole family to get stuck into the same meal. Family time at its finest!

1 tbsp olive oil

1 red onion, finely chopped

1 carrot, peeled and diced

4 garlic cloves, finely chopped

500g lean beef mince (5% fat)

600ml semi-skimmed milk

220g macaroni

1 packet Spaghetti Bolognese seasoning mix (I use Colman's)

1 x 400g tin chopped tomatoes

1 tbsp dried oregano

150g light mature Cheddar, grated

salt and pepper

400g crunchy salad (see Sides, page 209)

Low calorie switch:

unsweetened almond milk or skimmed milk

1. Preheat the oven to 240°C/220°C fan/gas 9.

2. Place a large pan over a medium heat. Add the olive oil, then add the onion and carrot and cook for 5–6 minutes.

3. Add the garlic, mince, salt and plenty of pepper and cook until browned.

4. Place the milk in a large pan and bring to the boil. Add the macaroni to the boiling milk and stir until the milk has almost evaporated and the macaroni is cooked.

5. Add the bolognese seasoning, tomatoes and oregano to the pan with the mince.

6. Turn off the heat under the macaroni and add 100g of the cheese – mix well until the cheese has melted. Add some freshly ground black pepper and mix well.

7. Place the mince mixture in an ovenproof dish.

8. Spoon the mac 'n' cheese on top, then sprinkle with the remaining cheese.

9. Bake for 10–15 minutes until golden and crispy. Serve immediately, with a crunchy side salad.

Serves 4 | **Nutrition** | 563 calories | 49g protein | 66g carbs | 8g fat

CHEESEBURGER LASAGNE

Those of you who have been following me for a while know that I love recreating something and throwing 'cheeseburger' in front of it!

A hearty meal for the family, and my goodness it is tasty. Given that this one isn't too difficult, it could be a way to get the kids involved in cooking: you could have them helping to stir the mince or pouring in the sauces. It's also a great one to prep ahead, giving you an easy meal later in the week.

Add some Worcestershire sauce to the lasagne for a little kick.

10–12 sprays light cooking oil

1 onion, chopped

500g lean beef mince (5% fat)

1 tbsp onion salt

1 tbsp garlic powder

1 tin condensed tomato soup

2 tbsp burger relish (I use Gourmet Burger Kitchen)

6 lasagne sheets (160g)

1 x 470g jar light lasagne white sauce (I use Dolmio)

60g Red Leicester, grated

6 gherkins, diced

1 tsp sesame seeds

400g crunchy salad (see Sides, page 209)

1. Preheat the oven to 210°C/190°C fan/gas 6½.

2. Heat a pan over a medium heat and spray with cooking oil, then add the onion and cook for 3–4 minutes until softened.

3. Add the mince, onion salt and garlic powder and cook until the mince is no longer pink.

4. Mix in the tomato soup and the burger relish.

5. Put half the mixture into an ovenproof dish, followed by half the lasagne sheets and half the white sauce.

6. Add the remaining mince mixture, followed by the rest of the lasagne sheets and the remaining white sauce.

7. Sprinkle the grated cheese over the top and bake for 20 minutes.

8. To finish, scatter the gherkins and sesame seeds on top. Serve with a crunchy side salad.

Serves 4 **Nutrition** | 575 calories | 37g protein | 58g carbs | 23g fat

HEARTY VEGGIE CHILLI

A top-class vegan chilli that delivers a healthy 36 grams of protein for 450 calories. Soya mince is a great high protein meat substitute, and it blends well with the other ingredients in this dish. Follow the instructions on the packet of soya mince. It may need to be soaked in water for up to 15 minutes before going into the mix.

If you're having a wee treat, get some tacos or tortilla chips involved here. I love scooping up the chilli and wolfing it down on a crisp.

This can be served immediately for the family, or chilli is of course a brilliant option for meal prepping. Once cool, the chilli will freeze for up to a month.

6 vegan sausages

10–20 sprays light cooking oil

1 onion, finely chopped

1 red pepper, cut into bite-sized chunks

4 garlic cloves, finely chopped

1 tsp chilli flakes

1 tbsp chilli powder

2 tbsp tomato purée

300g soya mince, soaked if necessary (see packet instructions)

2 x 400g tins chopped tomatoes

1 x 400g tin kidney beans, drained

3 tbsp vegan gravy granules

1 tbsp cocoa powder

salt and pepper

4 slices crusty tiger bread

Low calorie switch:
low calorie bread

1. Preheat the grill to medium-hot and grill the sausages for 10–12 minutes or until cooked through.

2. Meanwhile, heat a pan over a medium heat and spray it with cooking oil. Add the onion and cook for 3–4 minutes until softened.

3. Add the red pepper, garlic, chilli flakes, chilli powder, tomato purée, salt and pepper and stir well for 2 minutes.

4. Add the soya mince and cook for a further 5–6 minutes.

5. Pour in the chopped tomatoes, kidney beans, gravy granules and cocoa powder.

6. Chop up the sausages and add them to the mixture. Bring to the boil, then reduce the heat and simmer for 25 minutes.

7. Serve immediately, with crusty bread.

Serves 4

Nutrition | 450 calories | 36g protein | 54g carbs | 7g fat

CREAMY MEATBALLS

This is my twist on some classic Swedish meatballs. Don't worry, they don't come flat-packed, but you do get a handy set of instructions.

We've got these absolutely packed with protein. They could work as a snack at any time of day, as they taste great even when cold. The meatballs are very versatile: if you freeze them without the gravy, there are loads of options for serving them with other sauces.

If going for the whole hog and having these with the gravy, mashed potatoes or sweet potato mash are my go-to options as a side, along with some runner beans.

2 slices low calorie bread, crusts removed, chopped into chunks
3 tbsp semi-skimmed milk
1 onion, finely chopped
250g lean beef mince (5% fat)
250g lean pork mince (5% fat)
1 egg, beaten
½ tsp grated nutmeg
½ tsp ground allspice
8–10 sprays light cooking oil
salt and pepper
600g mashed potatoes (see Sides, page 210)

Gravy
1 tbsp light unsalted butter
2 tbsp plain flour
500ml beef stock
125ml single cream

1. Preheat the oven to 200°C/180°C fan/gas 6.
2. To a large bowl, add the bread, milk and onion. Mix well, then leave for 5 minutes to allow the bread to become soggy.
3. Add the beef and pork mince, egg, nutmeg, allspice, salt, pepper and combine well.
4. Using your hands, roll the mixture into 25–30 meatballs.
5. Heat a pan over a medium heat and spray with cooking oil. Add the meatballs and brown on all sides.
6. Place on a baking tray and bake for 10 minutes or until fully cooked through.

7. To make the gravy, add the butter to the pan in which you browned the meatballs. When it has melted, add the flour and stir continuously for 1 minute.
8. Add half the beef stock, stirring continuously. Gradually add the remaining beef stock, stirring to ensure there are no lumps left.
9. Bring the liquid to a simmer, then add the meatballs and simmer for 5–6 minutes, stirring continuously.
10. Add the cream and heat through for 2 minutes. Serve immediately, with mashed potatoes.

Serves 4

Nutrition | 486 calories | 38g protein | 36g carbs | 20g fat

BEEF STROGANOFF

An all-time classic, and a dish I just can't get enough of. A few small tweaks bring it in at a healthy calorie total so you can enjoy it time after time. If you've got any sauce left, don't be shy in soaking it up with a big hearty slice of fluffy bread ... bliss!

This can also be made with lean mince for a cheaper alternative. For a vegetarian version, some meat-free high protein mince works perfectly too.

500g sirloin steak, cut into strips
2 tbsp smoked paprika
1 tbsp cornflour
2 tbsp light butter
1 onion, finely chopped
400g mushrooms, sliced
4 garlic cloves, finely chopped
1 tbsp Dijon mustard
1 tbsp Worcestershire sauce
50g light soft cheese
300ml boiling beef stock
2 tbsp double cream
handful of fresh parsley, roughly chopped
salt and pepper
600g mashed potatoes (see Sides, page 210)
400g steamed broccoli

Low calorie switch:
leafy salad

1. In a large bowl combine the steak, 1 tablespoon of the smoked paprika, the cornflour, salt and pepper.
2. Heat a frying pan over a medium-high heat, then add 1 tablespoon of the butter and fry the steak for 2 minutes on each side. Remove from the pan and set aside.
3. Add the remaining butter to the pan, then add the onion and cook until softened.

4. Add the mushrooms and garlic and cook for a further 6 minutes.
5. Add the mustard, the remaining smoked paprika, the Worcestershire sauce, soft cheese and beef stock. Cover the pan and cook until the sauce thickens.
6. Put the steak back in the pan and finish with the cream and a sprinkle of parsley.
7. Serve with mashed potatoes and broccoli.

Serves 4 | **Nutrition** | 508 calories | 51g protein | 43g carbs | 15g fat

CHUNKY SAUSAGE CASSEROLE

Everyone loves a hearty casserole. For me, this is a weekend dish, or one where you have a reasonable amount of time, as I would expect this to take around 90 minutes from start to finish. That said, it's everything you need in a meal, so once it's done, so are you.

Golden rule is the chef doesn't have to wash up, right?

10–12 sprays light cooking oil

8 sausages (97% pork)

1 onion, chopped

2 garlic cloves, crushed

1 tbsp paprika

1 tbsp dried oregano

800g potatoes, peeled and cut into chunks

4 carrots, peeled and cut into chunks

1 x 400g tin chopped tomatoes

400ml hot vegetable stock

1–2 bay leaves

1. Preheat the oven to 200°C/180°C fan/gas 6.

2. Spray a flameproof casserole with the cooking oil and place over a medium-high heat. Add the sausages and brown for 10 minutes, turning them often.

3. Remove the sausages and set aside. Add the onion and cook until softened.

4. Add the garlic, paprika and oregano and cook for 2 minutes, then add the potatoes and carrots and mix well.

5. Add the tomatoes, stock and bay leaves. Bring to a simmer, then put the sausages back in.

6. Bake in the oven for 45 minutes. Serve hot.

TIP: Make this meal veggie or vegan simply by subbing out the sausages for a high protein, meat-free version.

Serves 4

Nutrition | 598 calories | 30g protein | 46g carbs | 31g fat

MUM'S FISH STEW

Plenty of ingredients in the list, but with a little organisation you'll be sorted in no time. Four hearty servings, and the time invested is more than worth it for the taste. In short, this meal is healthy and delicious. We're getting those good fatty acids from the fish and a massive 57 grams of protein per serving, so this will keep the hunger cravings at bay.

The wine in the sauce always seems to make it a bit special. This also has the bonus of all being cooked in the one pot – less washing up!

10–12 sprays light cooking oil

1 onion, finely diced

2 yellow peppers, cut into chunks

60g sun-dried tomatoes, roughly chopped

3 garlic cloves, crushed

3cm fresh root ginger, peeled and finely grated

1 tbsp paprika

1 tbsp dried oregano

1 tsp cayenne pepper

200ml dry white wine

2 x 400g tins chopped tomatoes

1 tbsp zero calorie sweetener

2 fresh rosemary sprigs, leaves roughly chopped

2 bay leaves

200g mussels

350g cod loin, cut into chunks

400g raw tiger prawns

juice of ½ lime

handful of fresh parsley, roughly chopped

salt and pepper

4 slices crusty tiger bread

1. Heat a large pan over a medium heat and spray with the cooking oil. Add the onion and cook for 5–6 minutes until softened.

2. Add the peppers, sun-dried tomatoes, garlic, ginger, paprika, oregano and cayenne pepper and cook for 4 minutes.

3. Pour in the white wine and simmer until reduced by half.

4. Add the chopped tomatoes, sweetener, rosemary and bay leaves, then bring to a gentle simmer.

5. Season with salt and pepper, then cover the pan and simmer for 45 minutes.

6. Meanwhile, scrub the mussels and wash in several changes of water, discarding any broken shells and any that do not close when firmly tapped.

7. Remove the tomato mixture from the heat and blitz with a hand blender until smooth.

8. Return to the heat and bring to the boil, then add the mussels and cook for a minute or two until the shells open.

9. Add the cod and prawns and cook for a further 4 minutes until the fish and prawns are cooked through.

10. Add the lime juice and scatter the parsley over the top. Serve with crusty bread and get dipping.

Low calorie switch:
low calorie bread or sandwich thin

Serves 4

Nutrition | 538 calories | 57g protein | 48g carbs | 10g fat

CHICKEN and LEEK PIE

In an ideal world I would be eating this as a late Sunday lunch surrounded by the family. Not a lot of ingredients for this one: it's a hassle-free pie with no pastry in sight and it hits all the macro targets. Pour yourself a little glass of wine, put on some of your favourite music and get cooking.

1kg potatoes, peeled and cut into large chunks
10–12 sprays light cooking oil
600g skinless chicken breast, chopped into chunks
4 large leeks, sliced
1 tin condensed chicken soup
1 tbsp light butter
100g light Cheddar cheese, grated
salt and pepper
320g steamed fine green beans

1. Preheat the oven to 200°C/180°C fan/gas 6.

2. Put the potatoes in a large pot, add water to cover and bring to the boil. Simmer for 15–20 minutes or until soft enough to mash.

3. Meanwhile, heat a pan over a medium heat and spray with cooking oil. Add the chicken and cook until browned.

4. Add the leeks, cover the pan and cook until the leeks are soft.

5. Pour the chicken soup into the chicken and leek mixture and stir well. Put this mixture into an ovenproof dish.

6. Drain the potatoes, add the butter and some salt and pepper and mash well.

7. Gently spread the mash over the chicken mixture, then sprinkle the cheese on top.

8. Bake for 15–20 minutes until golden brown and crispy.

9. Serve with steamed green beans.

Serves 4 | **Nutrition** | 483 calories | 47g protein | 47g carbs | 11g fat

FISH PIE

Our family grew up on this. I've given it a twist by adding fresh dill and using half-fat crème fraîche, so we're ticking those calorie goal boxes. As you would expect, this is a go-to if you're cooking for the family or a crowd. Although be warned, you'd be best cooking extras! It's easy to multiply the ingredients up to serve 6 or 8, but you'll need a bigger dish.

400g potatoes, peeled and chopped

400g sweet potatoes, peeled and chopped

2 eggs

20g light unsalted butter

1 onion, chopped

100ml light crème fraîche

420g skinless haddock fillets

1 tsp English mustard

2 tbsp freshly chopped dill

salt and pepper

1 tsp fresh chives, finely snipped

320g medley of green veg (see Sides, page 211)

1. Preheat the oven to 220°C/200°C fan/gas 7.

2. Bring a large pan of water to the boil and put the potatoes and sweet potato in to cook.

3. Pop the eggs in another pan to boil.

4. In another pan, melt the butter and gently fry the onion for 3–4 minutes until softened.

5. Add the crème fraîche and bring to a simmer. Add the haddock and simmer gently for 6–7 minutes or until it starts to flake apart.

6. When the potatoes are soft, drain and mash them. Season with salt and pepper to taste.

7. Peel the eggs, chop and add to the mashed potatoes.

8. Stir in the mustard and dill.

9. Put the haddock mixture into an ovenproof dish. Spread the mash over the top, then bake for 8 minutes until golden brown.

10. Sprinkle with chives and serve immediately, with a medley of green veg.

Serves 4 | **Nutrition** | 504 calories | 50g protein | 43g carbs | 14g fat

COTTAGE PIE

A classic in every household, this'll have the kids and their friends running to the table. This is also a good one for doubling up the ingredients if you like being prepped for the week ahead.

If you are cooking for kids, you could add some more vegetables if you normally struggle to convince them. Sweetcorn is a good choice here.

For a vegetarian version, use meat-free mince, onion gravy and vegetable stock.

800g potatoes, peeled and cut into large chunks
10–12 sprays light cooking oil
500g lean beef mince (5% fat)
1 onion, finely chopped
2 carrots, peeled and diced
200g green beans, cut into 2cm pieces
250ml beef stock
2 tbsp Worcestershire sauce
4 tbsp gravy granules
2 tbsp tomato purée
10g light butter
100g light mozzarella, chopped into chunks
salt and pepper
320g medley of green veg (see Sides, page 211)

1. Preheat the oven to 240°C/220°C fan/gas 9.

2. Put the potatoes in a large pot, add water to cover and bring to the boil. Simmer for 15–20 minutes or until soft enough to mash.

3. Meanwhile, heat a pan over a medium heat and spray with cooking oil. Add the mince and cook until browned.

4. Add the onion, carrots and green beans and gently fry for 3–4 minutes.

5. Mix in the beef stock, Worcestershire sauce, gravy granules and tomato purée. You may need to add a little hot water, but the idea is to create a thick mixture.

6. Put the mixture into an ovenproof dish.

7. Drain the potatoes, add the butter and some salt and pepper and mash well.

8. Gently spread the mash over the mince mixture, then scatter the cheese on top.

9. Bake for 6–10 minutes until the cheese has melted and begun to brown.

10. Serve with a medley of green vegetables.

Serves 4

Nutrition | 483 calories | 41g protein | 47g carbs | 11g fat

CHICKEN *and* CHORIZO PIE

This might be something new for the family. With both chicken and chorizo, it's packed with protein, and it won't let you down in the taste department either. It might look like there are a lot of ingredients, but it's actually pretty straightforward to cook. You can get away with one large frying pan and one baking dish, so there's not even a lot of washing up.

I'm sure that this is one you will love. Served with a side of vegetables or potatoes it's the perfect evening or late lunch meal, though if you go for potatoes this will change the calorie and macro counts.

1 packet (212g) puff pastry
8–10 sprays light cooking oil
80g chorizo, cubed
600g chicken, chopped into chunks
1 onion, finely chopped
1 red pepper, diced
1 tbsp paprika
1 tbsp garlic powder
1 tbsp tomato purée
1 tbsp dried oregano
500g cherry tomatoes, halved
handful of basil, roughly chopped
120ml single cream
½ egg, beaten
320g medley of green veg (see Sides, page 211)

1. Preheat the oven to 220°C/ 200°C fan/gas 7.
2. Open the puff pastry packet and set to one side.
3. Heat a large frying pan over a medium heat and spray with cooking oil. Add the chorizo and cook until crispy, then remove from the pan, leaving as much oil in the pan as possible.
4. Add the chicken to the pan and fry for 8–10 minutes.
5. Add the onion, red pepper, paprika and garlic powder and gently fry for a further 3–4 minutes.
6. Mix in the tomato purée, oregano and cherry tomatoes and cook for an additional 2 minutes.

7. Sprinkle in the basil, followed by the cooked chorizo and cream.
8. Put the mixture into an ovenproof dish.
9. Roll out the pastry to cover the dish. Trim the edges.
10. Brush the pastry with the beaten egg and pop it in the oven for 15 minutes or until golden brown and crispy.
11. Serve with a medley of green vegetables.

Serves 4 | **Nutrition** | 593 calories | 50g protein | 37g carbs | 27g fat

PROTEIN-PACKED STEAK PIE

The New Year's Eve classic. Or should it be the first day of the New Year classic? Either way, this is a cracking option for a fancy occasion. If you are expecting a lot of guests, you can double everything up and use two dishes – or one big dish.

Keep an eye on the pastry when this is in the oven, as you don't want to go through all the effort of making the steak mixture only for it to burn at the end.

1 tbsp olive oil

500g braising beef, cut into even-sized chunks

1 large red onion

1 large carrot, peeled and diced

3 garlic cloves, finely chopped

200g mushrooms, chopped

3 fresh thyme sprigs, leaves picked

2 tbsp plain flour

2 tbsp tomato purée

150ml red wine

350ml beef stock

1 tbsp Worcestershire sauce

1 packet (212g) puff pastry

½ egg, beaten

salt and pepper

400g steamed broccoli

1. Preheat the oven to 180°C/160°C fan/gas 4.

2. In a large flameproof lidded casserole, heat the oil over a medium heat, add the beef and brown on all sides for 4–5 minutes. Remove and set aside.

3. In the same pan add the onion, carrot and garlic and cook for 3–4 minutes.

4. Add the mushrooms and thyme and season well with salt and pepper.

5. Add the flour and tomato purée, stirring well for 1 minute.

6. Put the beef back into the pan and add the red wine, beef stock and Worcestershire sauce. Bring to a gentle simmer, then cover with the lid and place in the oven for 1¼ hours.

7. Remove the casserole from the oven. Turn the oven up to 200°C/180°C fan/gas 6.

8. Roll out the pastry to a little larger than your ovenproof dish or pie tin. Add the cooked beef mixture to the dish and then cover with the pastry. Trim the edges.

9. Brush the pastry with the beaten egg and bake for 20 minutes or until golden brown on top.

10. Serve with broccoli.

Serves 4

Nutrition | 549 calories | 39g protein | 42g carbs | 28g fat

DAUPHINOISE CHICKEN PIE

I have always loved Dauphinoise potatoes but the skill of cooking them properly was beyond my reach for a while. Thankfully, I think I've now got it cracked. In this recipe I've combined them with chicken to pack a punch in the protein department. This meal delivers 49 grams of protein for 514 calories, so it's a perfect choice for anyone looking to cut down on their body fat.

500g potatoes, thinly sliced
150ml semi-skimmed milk
150ml single cream
2 garlic cloves, peeled
2 bay leaves
4 fresh thyme sprigs
10–20 sprays light cooking oil
600g skinless chicken breast, cut into chunks
200g mushrooms, halved
1 leek, finely sliced
1 tin condensed mushroom soup
20g Parmesan, grated
1 tsp grated nutmeg
salt and pepper
400g steamed broccoli

1. Preheat the oven to 220°C/200°C fan/gas 7.

2. Put the potatoes in a large pan with the milk, cream, garlic, bay leaves and thyme. Bring to the boil, then remove from the heat and set aside.

3. Heat a pan over a medium heat and spray with cooking oil. Add the chicken and brown for 8–10 minutes, then remove and set aside.

4. Spray the pan with some more cooking oil, then gently fry the mushrooms and leek for 10 minutes until soft.

5. Add the mushroom soup and the chicken, season with salt and pepper and mix well.

6. Put the mix in an ovenproof dish.

7. Spoon the potato mixture on top and sprinkle with the Parmesan and nutmeg.

8. Cover the dish with foil and bake for 45 minutes.

9. Remove the foil, then bake for a further 20–25 minutes or until the potatoes are tender when tested with a skewer.

10. Serve immediately, with broccoli.

Serves 4 | **Nutrition** | 514 calories | 49g protein | 39g carbs | 19g fat

FAKEAWAY

CHICKEN PAD THAI

When I was travelling in Thailand as a backpacker, this was my one special meal of the day. When I say I ate this for 36 consecutive nights, I really mean it – I regret nothing, other than perhaps not having it for breakfast as well as dinner – and therefore it was only right to include it in this book. Not only is this a total cracker of a dish, it's also fairly simple to make, so don't be put off by the ingredients list: everything contributes to the flavour.

At just 471 calories and a whopping 46 grams of protein, this is one to enjoy over and over again.

5 tbsp light soy sauce

2 tbsp oyster sauce

2 tbsp tamarind paste

2 tbsp fish sauce

1 tbsp zero calorie brown sugar alternative (I use Pure Via)

juice of 2 limes

600g skinless chicken, cut into chunks

1 tbsp garlic powder

1 tsp cayenne pepper

1 tsp ground black pepper

2 tsp olive oil

2 shallots, finely diced

4 garlic cloves, finely chopped

5–6 spring onions, cut into long strips

300g flat rice noodles, cooked to the packet instructions

2 eggs, lightly beaten

1 tbsp crushed peanuts

1 lime, cut into quarters

1. Start by making the sauce: combine 3 tablespoons of the soy sauce, 1 tablespoon of the oyster sauce, the tamarind paste, fish sauce, brown sugar and half the lime juice and mix well. Set aside.

2. In a large bowl, combine the chicken with the remaining soy sauce, oyster sauce and lime juice, the garlic powder, cayenne and black pepper.

3. Heat a large pan over a medium heat, add 1 teaspoon of the olive oil and fry the chicken until cooked through and golden brown. Remove from the pan and set aside.

4. To the same pan, add the remaining olive oil, the shallots, garlic and spring onions and cook for 1 minute.

5. Add the cooked noodles followed by the sauce mixture.

6. Push the ingredients to one side of the pan, then add the eggs. Mix so they begin to scramble, then combine with the noodle mixture.

7. Put the chicken back in the pan and mix well.

8. To serve, sprinkle the peanuts on top and add lime quarters on the side to squeeze over the dish. For a bit of extra crunch, you could toast the nuts.

Serves 4 **Nutrition** | 471 calories | 46g protein | 52g carbs | 8g fat

CRISPY CHILLI BEEF

My twist on this classic dish, and one that is really easy to adjust to your own taste. I like to load my dishes with vegetables where possible, so do experiment with this one and see what works for you. If you're looking to add calories, this is a great dish for throwing in some cashew nuts and frying them with the beef.

Another idea, if you like to spice up your life, is to fire in some more chilli for that extra kick. Don't go crazy on this front though, I nearly burnt my tongue off the first time I tried it!

Nutritious, quick and tasty – a great midweek meal.

300g thin-cut minute steak, cut into strips
2 tbsp cornflour
2 tsp Chinese five spice
1 tbsp vegetable oil
1 red pepper, thinly sliced
1 red chilli, thinly sliced
1 tbsp chilli flakes
4 spring onions, sliced
2 garlic cloves, crushed
4cm fresh root ginger, peeled and grated
3 tbsp white wine vinegar
1 tbsp soy sauce
2 tbsp light sweet chilli sauce
2 tbsp tomato ketchup
2 tsp zero calorie white sweetener
1 packet microwave basmati rice (250g cooked weight)

Low calorie switch:
konjac rice or cauliflower rice

1. Put the beef in a bowl, add the cornflour and five spice and give it a good toss.
2. Heat the oil in a wok or large frying pan until hot, then add the beef and stir-fry until golden and crisp. Remove the beef from the pan and set aside.
3. In the same pan add the red pepper, chilli, chilli flakes, spring onions, garlic and ginger and stir-fry for 2–3 minutes.

4. In a bowl, mix together the white wine vinegar, soy sauce, sweet chilli sauce, ketchup and sweetener with 2 tablespoons of water, then pour over the veg in the pan.
5. Gently simmer for 2 minutes until the sauce starts to thicken, then add the beef back into the pan and toss well.
6. Serve with basmati rice.

Serves 2 | **Nutrition** | 531 calories | 35g protein | 70g carbs | 12g fat

CHILLI GARLIC KING PRAWNS

Chilli Garlic Prawns, there's three words that go together well. And now there is no need to leave the house or to wait for the delivery. Coming in at only 416 calories, this will have you enjoying all those takeaway feels without any guilt – not that you should ever feel guilt for eating.

I'm serving mine with rice but this would also work really well with noodles.

350g raw king prawns, peeled and deveined
1 tbsp cornflour
1 tsp smoked paprika
1 tsp sesame oil
2 tbsp light soy sauce
2 tbsp sriracha sauce
3 tbsp zero calorie brown sugar alternative (I use Pure Via)
1 tbsp honey
1 tsp white rice vinegar
1 chilli, finely chopped
1 tbsp chilli flakes
1 tbsp garlic powder
2 spring onions, finely chopped
salt and pepper
1 packet microwave jasmine rice (250g cooked weight)

Low calorie switch:
konjac rice, cauliflower rice or courgette spaghetti (see Sides, page 209)

1. Pat the prawns dry with kitchen paper.
2. In a bowl combine the cornflour and smoked paprika with some salt and pepper. Add the prawns and toss until the prawns are evenly coated.
3. Heat a frying pan over a medium heat, add the sesame oil, then fry the prawns for 1 minute. Remove from the heat.
4. In a bowl combine the soy sauce, sriracha, brown sugar, honey, vinegar, chilli, chilli flakes and garlic powder and mix well.
5. Add the mixture to the prawns and return to the heat for 2 minutes until the sauce thickens.
6. Garnish with spring onions and serve over jasmine rice.

TIP: Switching the white rice for brown is an even healthier option!

Serves 2 | **Nutrition** | 416 calories | 32g protein | 60g carbs | 5g fat

SOYA CHUNK KUNG PAO

This vegan dish is a spicy little number that hits the protein targets. Lots of flavour in this one and it would be one of my top choices if you're cooking for someone who enjoys a little spice in their food.

This is also a good one to consider for doubling up the ingredients for advance meal prep. It's fantastic reheated as an office lunch.

Look for high protein soya chunks for this recipe. There are some options out there with 45–50% protein, so they're ideal. I like jasmine rice here but it's down to personal preference – basmati rice or whatever you like will work grand.

120g soya chunks

350ml hot vegetable stock

1 tbsp light soy sauce

2 tsp bicarbonate of soda

1 tsp cornflour

2 tsp sesame oil

2 red peppers, cut into strips

4 spring onions, chopped into 2cm pieces

3 garlic cloves, roughly chopped

1 tbsp cashew nuts, roughly chopped

1 packet microwave jasmine rice (250g cooked weight)

Sauce

1 tbsp dark soy sauce

100ml vegetable stock

1 tsp cornflour

2 garlic cloves, finely chopped

3cm fresh root ginger, peeled and finely grated

5 tbsp light soy sauce

1 tbsp white wine vinegar

1 tbsp hoisin sauce

1. Soak the soya chunks in the hot vegetable stock for 10 minutes.

2. Make the sauce by combining all the ingredients in a small bowl.

3. Drain any excess liquid from the soya chunks – you might want to squeeze them out using a spatula – then toss in a bowl with the light soy sauce, bicarbonate of soda and cornflour.

4. Heat a wok or large frying pan over a medium heat, add 1 teaspoon of the sesame oil, then add the soya chunks and stir-fry for 6 minutes until golden brown on all sides. Remove from the pan and set aside.

5. In the same pan add the remaining sesame oil and the peppers and stir-fry for 3 minutes.

6. Add the spring onions, garlic and cashew nuts and cook for a further 2 minutes.

7. Add the sauce to the pan, followed by the soya chunks, and stir to combine all the ingredients.

8. Serve with jasmine rice.

Serves 2 | **Nutrition** | 485 calories | 20g protein | 70g carbs | 14g fat

CHICKEN BIRYANI

Two words to describe this dish – flavour and aroma. I'm going to add two more – pure joy – as this dish deserves it. One of my favourite things in the whole wide world is cooking rice with a range of different spices. There's a famous girl band who said 'spice up your life' and that's exactly what we're doing with this masterclass of flavours.

The great thing about this dish is it tastes even better the next day (if it lasts that long), once the flavours have combined further. Work lunch sorted!

600g skinless chicken breast, diced
200g fat-free Greek-style yoghurt
1½ tbsp garam masala
5 garlic cloves, finely chopped
1 tbsp ginger purée
1 tbsp chilli powder
1 tbsp turmeric
1 tbsp olive oil
2 onions, thinly sliced
1 tsp ground cinnamon
1 tsp ground cumin
200g uncooked basmati rice
1 x 400g tin chopped tomatoes
500ml boiling chicken stock
handful of fresh coriander, roughly chopped

Rice spices

1 tsp turmeric
1 tbsp garam masala
1 tbsp chilli powder

1. Put the chicken in a large bowl with the yoghurt, garam masala, garlic, ginger, chilli powder and turmeric. Leave in the fridge to marinate overnight for the best flavour, or if time's tight, allow 1 hour.

2. Heat a pan over a medium heat, add the olive oil and then the chicken and fry for 8–10 minutes until cooked through. Remove the chicken from the pan and set to one side.

3. Add the onions to the pan, followed by the cinnamon and cumin, and cook until softened.

4. Add the rice spices and then the rice and stir to coat the rice in the spices.

5. Add the chopped tomatoes and the chicken stock, bring to a simmer, then cover and cook for 15 minutes until the rice is tender.

6. Put the chicken back in the pan and mix well.

7. Serve immediately, scattered with coriander.

Serves 4 | **Nutrition** | 479 calories | 50g protein | 55g carbs | 8g fat

TIP: It may or may not taste that little bit better alongside a cool glass of beer ...

DIRTY FRIES

They may look like a side but these bad boys can be a main dish. Not too many calories at 503 per serving – even with cheese – and packed with a booming 46 grams of protein per serving, they're perfect for weekend relaxing or even during a training regime.

If you want to make it healthier, you can leave out the cheese to bring down the calories. Not something I have ever done if I'm honest. If you're going dirty, get dirty!

Serve with roasted veg as a side.

900g potatoes, scrubbed and cut into wedges
12–20 sprays light cooking oil
1 red onion, finely chopped
4 garlic cloves, finely chopped
500g lean beef mince (5% fat)
3 tbsp barbecue seasoning (I use Schwartz)
1 tbsp chilli flakes
1 x 400g tin chopped tomatoes
5–6 spring onions, finely chopped
4 tbsp barbecue sauce
100g light Cheddar, grated
salt and pepper

1. Preheat the oven to 220°C/200°C fan/gas 7.
2. Bring a large pan of salted water to the boil and put the potato wedges in to cook for 8 minutes.
3. Heat a pan over a medium heat and spray with cooking oil, then add the onion and garlic and cook for 3 minutes.
4. Add the mince and fry, stirring, until browned.
5. Drain the potatoes and pat dry, then coat them with 1 tablespoon of the barbecue seasoning and the chilli flakes.
6. Place them in a baking tray, season with salt and pepper and lightly spray with oil.

7. Pop into the oven for 15 minutes.
8. Add the remaining barbecue seasoning to the mince and then mix in the chopped tomatoes, stirring well.
9. Add the spring onions and stir in half the barbecue sauce.
10. After 15 minutes, take the potato wedges out of the oven and pour the mince mixture on top, adding the remaining barbecue sauce.
11. Sprinkle the cheese on top and pop back into the oven to melt the cheese.
12. Serve immediately.

Serves 4 **Nutrition** | 503 calories | 46g protein | 48g carbs | 15g fat

The ULTIMATE NACHOS

Nachos aren't just for the cinema! They're lovely as a shared snack with friends. With the jalapeños these have a little kick, but skip these if you'd rather take off some of the heat. Packed with protein and coming in at only 483 calories, it's win-win-win here.

This one can take a little time to perfect, so don't rush and it'll taste all the better.

10–12 sprays light cooking oil
500g lean beef mince (5% fat)
1 tsp chilli powder
1 tsp ground cumin
1 tbsp paprika
1 tbsp garlic powder
1 x 400g tin chopped tomatoes
170g tortilla crisps
70g light mozzarella, chopped into chunks
10–12 jalapeños
3 tbsp light soured cream
salt and pepper

Home-made salsa
4 tomatoes, diced
1 tsp garlic purée
juice of ½ lime
½ red onion, finely chopped

Low calorie switch:
low calorie tortilla crisps

1. Preheat the oven to 180°C/160°C fan/gas 4.
2. For the salsa, combine the tomatoes, garlic purée, lime juice and onion, then set aside.
3. Heat a pan over a medium heat and spray with cooking oil, then add the mince and break up the mince with a wooden spoon.
4. Add the chilli powder, cumin, paprika, garlic powder, salt and pepper and let the mince brown for 8–10 minutes.
5. Add the chopped tomatoes and cook for a further 2 minutes.
6. Put the tortilla crisps into a large ovenproof dish and heat in the oven for 4 minutes.

7. Once heated, remove a third of the crisps, then spoon half the mince mixture on top, followed by half the mozzarella and half the salsa.
8. Repeat this process with the remaining crisps, mince, salsa and cheese.
9. Add the jalapeños, then bake for 6–8 minutes or until golden brown.
10. To finish, add the soured cream and serve immediately.

Serves 4

Nutrition | 483 calories | 37g protein | 40g carbs | 20g fat

VEGAN BURGER BAGEL

A vegan twist on the classic cheeseburger, and incredibly simple to make. One for the barbecue with friends, something to entertain the kids, or just a treat for yourself. It has everything the original has – except the meat! Meat-free mince is super-easy to cook and packed with protein.

Double up the amount of 'meat mix' and keep in the fridge to make meatballs later in the week.

125g meat-free mince

1 tsp olive oil

1 tsp onion salt

1 tsp garlic powder

10–12 sprays light cooking oil

1 slice light plant-based cheese

½ red onion, thinly sliced

1 tsp zero calorie brown sugar alternative (I use Pure Via)

1 thin bagel (I use Warburtons Protein Thins), split and lightly toasted

40g gherkins, sliced

mixed leafy salad (see Sides, page 209)

Sauce

1 tbsp light mayonnaise

1 tsp gherkin relish

1 tsp English mustard

1 tsp white wine vinegar

1 tsp zero calorie sweetener

1 tsp onion granules

1 tsp garlic powder

1 tsp paprika

Low calorie switch:
sandwich thin

1. Combine the mince with the olive oil, onion salt and garlic powder and mix well, then form into a burger patty shape.

2. Heat a pan over a medium heat and spray with cooking oil, then gently fry the burger for 10–12 minutes, turning occasionally. Remove from the pan, lay the cheese slice on top and set aside.

3. Spray a little more oil into the pan, add the onion and cook for 6–8 minutes until softened, then add the brown sugar and 1 tablespoon of water.

4. While these are cooking, make the sauce by combining all the ingredients in a bowl.

5. To serve, spread half the sauce over the bottom half of the bagel. Add the cheese burger, then the gherkins and the remaining sauce. Finish with the top half of the bagel.

6. Serve immediately with a mixed leafy salad.

Serves 1

Nutrition | 513 calories | 28g protein | 57g carbs | 19g fat

The UPSIDE-DOWN BURGER

When I first heard about this I thought it was madness, and you might too. But trust me, give it a try and you'll be impressed. I wouldn't necessarily turn a burger upside-down on a first date – your date might run away – but you won't regret trying it out on other occasions. It's really easy to cook, though if you're not feeling too confident about creating your own burger patties, you could always opt for ready-made reduced fat burgers. I'll leave it in your hands, chef!

80g lean beef mince (5% fat)

1 tsp olive oil

1 tbsp onion granules

1 tbsp garlic powder

10–12 sprays light cooking oil

1 tbsp light mayonnaise

1 seeded brioche burger bun, split

½ white onion, finely sliced

1 tsp zero calorie brown sugar alternative (I use Pure Via)

2 cheese slices

1 tbsp tomato ketchup

1 tbsp mustard

mixed leafy salad (see Sides, page 209)

Low calorie switch:
sandwich thin, low calorie wrap or thin bagel

1. Combine the mince with the olive oil, onion granules and garlic powder and mix well. Roll the mixture into a ball shape.

2. Heat a frying pan over a medium heat and spray with cooking oil. Add the mince ball to the pan and press down firmly to create a burger shape.

3. Cook for 6–8 minutes on each side, then remove and set aside.

4. Meanwhile, spread the mayonnaise over both halves of the brioche bun and set aside.

5. Spray a little more oil into the frying pan, add the onion and cook until softened. Add the brown sugar and 1 tablespoon of water. Tip the onion onto a plate.

6. Put the brioche bun halves into the pan, mayonnaise side down.

7. Add one cheese slice to each half bun.

8. Add a burger to the seeded half of the bun and put the onion on top of the burger.

9. Add the tomato ketchup and mustard to the other half of the bun and then flip this over onto the burger.

10. Lift the burger onto a piece of foil, wrap and wait for 2–3 minutes or until the cheese has melted.

11. Serve with a mixed leafy salad.

Serves 1

Nutrition | 500 calories | 29g protein | 44g carbs | 24g fat

TIP: Don't eat this upside down!

BIG FRAZ SALAD

A salad in the fakeaway section? I hear ya, guys. Don't worry though, this is a real work of art and something you will be proud to show off to anyone. Salads are awesome in terms of the 'return', as we can enjoy a sizable amount of food for a fairly low calorie intake. I also feel that they're generally not the 'done thing' if you're ordering in a restaurant, so here's one you can enjoy at home.

As you would expect, just because it's a salad we're not shirking the protein targets. This meal will return a chunky 39 grams of protein for 366 calories. And the great thing about salads is they're so easy to prepare.

½ red onion, finely diced
2 tbsp pickles, finely diced
1 tbsp light mayonnaise
1 tbsp tomato ketchup
1 tsp English mustard
1 tsp paprika
1 tsp white wine vinegar
10–12 sprays light cooking oil
125g lean beef mince (5% fat)
1 tsp garlic powder
80g iceberg lettuce, shredded
20g light Cheddar, grated
1 tsp sesame seeds, toasted
salt and pepper

1. In a small bowl, make the sauce by combining 1 tablespoon of the red onion, 1 tablespoon of the pickles, the mayonnaise, ketchup, mustard, paprika and vinegar. Place in the fridge until required.

2. Heat a pan over a medium heat and spray with cooking oil, then add the mince and fry until browned. Season with salt, pepper and garlic powder, then remove from the heat and leave to cool.

3. Put the lettuce, the remaining red onion and pickles in a serving bowl. Add the mince and sauce mixture, then mix well.

4. Serve sprinkled with toasted sesame seeds.

TIP: An easy vegetarian switch by opting for high protein meatless mince.

Serves 1

Nutrition | 366 calories | 39g protein | 20g carbs | 15g fat

HEALTHIER FISH 'N' CHIPS

The classic British chippy. The meal that built a nation, and I absolutely love it. My twist on it is perfect for those of you who are keeping an eye on the calories or looking to hit protein goals.

There is no need to resist temptation with this variation: it is around half the calories of a standard fish 'n' chips takeaway meal.

You can get everyone involved in this. The kids will love helping to prep the fish and dipping it in the breadcrumbs, although I take no responsibility for the mess.

300g potatoes, peeled and cut into chip shapes

10–12 sprays light olive oil

80ml buttermilk

2 tbsp all-purpose seasoning (I use Schwartz)

2 haddock or cod fillets, skin removed

50g plain flour

1 tsp salt

60ml egg whites

70g panko breadcrumbs

2 tbsp malt vinegar

2 servings of mushy peas (see Sides, page 211)

1 lemon, cut into wedges

1. Preheat the oven to 220°C/200°C fan/gas 7. Line a large baking sheet with greaseproof paper.
2. Place the chips on the baking sheet, spray with some light olive oil and bake for 10 minutes.
3. Meanwhile, in a large bowl combine the buttermilk with 1 tablespoon of the all-purpose seasoning. Add the fish fillets and coat well.
4. Put the flour in a shallow dish and season with the salt.
5. In another shallow dish, whisk the egg whites until foamy.
6. In a third shallow dish, combine the panko breadcrumbs with the remaining all-purpose seasoning.
7. Remove the fish from the buttermilk and shake off any excess liquid.
8. Coat the fish in the flour, then dip it in the egg whites. Allow any excess egg to drip off before adding to the dish with the panko breadcrumbs. Press to coat the fish in the breadcrumbs.
9. Remove the baking sheet from the oven, then add the fish alongside the chips. Bake in the oven for 15 minutes or until the fish and chips are fully cooked through.
10. Remove the chips and toss in the malt vinegar.
11. Serve immediately, with mushy peas and lemon wedges.

Serves 2

Nutrition | 541 calories | 44g protein | 82g carbs | 4g fat

CHEESY CHIPOTLE STEAK TACOS

The day I discovered chipotle was the day everything in my life just got so much better. The grass was that wee bit greener, the sun that wee bit brighter. I mean, we all love a taco, but now we're taking things to a whole new level with chipotle flavours bursting through them.

Once you dip the taco into the mixture, then lightly char it, you're left with a flavour on the outside that's almost as good as the inside. Perfect for when you've got friends over or if you're looking to impress on date night – you can easily make this with half the quantities.

400g frying steak, cut into strips

2 tsp olive oil

1 red onion, finely diced

2 red peppers, cut into thin strips

2 tbsp chipotle paste

1 x 400g tin chopped tomatoes

8 soft taco wraps (I use Old El Paso) or mini wraps

80g light mozzarella, chopped into chunks

200g crunchy salad (see Sides, page 209)

Seasoning mix

1 tbsp dried oregano

1 tbsp chilli flakes

1 tbsp garlic powder

1 tbsp onion granules

½ tsp salt

½ tsp ground black pepper

1. Combine all the seasoning mix ingredients, then divide between two bowls. Toss the steak in half of the seasoning and 1 teaspoon of the olive oil.

2. Heat a pan over a high heat, add the steak and cook for 2 minutes. Remove from the pan and set aside.

3. To the same pan add the remaining olive oil followed by the onion, peppers, the surplus seasoning and the chipotle paste. Cook for 4 minutes until the veg are soft.

4. Add the chopped tomatoes and cook for a further 2 minutes.

5. Mix in the steak, then turn off the heat.

6. Preheat a large frying pan over a high heat. Dip one side of a taco wrap into the steak mixture, then lightly char in the hot frying pan for 1 minute.

7. Add ⅛ of the steak mixture onto one side of the wrap, followed by 10g of the mozzarella. Fold the wrap over and cook in the hot pan on both sides until the cheese has melted.

8. Repeat until you have made all the tacos. Serve immediately, with crunchy salad.

Serves 4 (2 tacos each)

Nutrition | 507 calories | 36g protein | 58g carbs | 17g fat

CHICKEN SOUVLAKI *with* TZATZIKI

My version of a top Greek dish. You can't go wrong with Greek food, there is so much to love about it. The tzatziki sauce is well suited to this recipe, but it is easy to make and works with a lot of different foods, so you might want to make double and keep it in the fridge for serving alongside salads, lamb kebabs or your favourite roasted veg. I'm also a huge fan of dipping some carrot batons into this vibrant tzatziki.

The kids will love the pitta bread here, and you can be sneaky and pack it with vegetables. For a vegetarian version, it works well with shredded omelette instead of chicken.

You will need 8 wooden kebab skewers.

700g skinless chicken breast, cut into large chunks
4 tbsp olive oil
2 garlic cloves, finely chopped
1 tbsp dried oregano
1 tbsp smoked paprika
1 tsp dried mint
juice of 2 lemons
4 pitta breads
1 head of lettuce, shredded
4 plum tomatoes, cut into chunks
1 small red onion, thinly sliced
1 lemon, cut into wedges
salt and pepper

Tzatziki
½ cucumber, cut into chunks
200g fat-free Greek-style yoghurt
small bunch of mint, finely chopped
1 garlic clove, finely chopped
2 tsp white wine vinegar

Low calorie switch: low calorie wrap

1. Put the chicken in a sandwich bag with 3 tablespoons of the olive oil, the garlic, oregano, smoked paprika, mint and lemon juice and leave in the fridge to marinate for 1–2 hours.
2. For the tzatziki, combine all the ingredients in a bowl, season with salt and pepper and mix well. Chill until ready to serve.
3. Soak the wooden skewers in water for 15 minutes.
4. Thread the chunks of chicken onto the skewers.

5. Preheat the grill to high or heat the barbecue.
6. Cook the chicken for 8–10 minutes, turning occasionally, until no longer pink in the centre.
7. Meanwhile, brush the pittas with the remaining olive oil and gently heat through in a pan over a medium heat or on the side of the barbecue.
8. Stuff the pittas with the chicken, lettuce, tomatoes and red onion and serve with lemon wedges.

Serves 4

Nutrition | 497 calories | 50g protein | 37g carbs | 17g fat

LAMB KEBABS

This is a Persian-inspired dish. Full of natural fresh ingredients, these kebabs are the incomparable healthy alternative to the takeaway kind. Once tried, you'll never look back. There are a few steps to getting this one just right, and you'll get better at it with practice, so don't worry if your first attempt isn't the finished article. It took me a few tries to master it, but now it's one of my favourites.

You can prepare the kebabs in advance, so this is ideal if you have some friends coming round. Perfect as part of a barbecue, with the sun overhead and a beer in hand.

You will need 8 wooden kebab skewers.

1 tbsp olive oil
1 red onion, finely chopped
3 garlic cloves, chopped
250g lean lamb mince (10% fat)
250g lean beef mince (5% fat)
1 tsp ground cumin
1 tsp hot paprika
1 tsp Chinese five spice
1 tsp dried oregano
1 tbsp tomato purée
grated zest of 1 lemon
10–12 sprays light cooking oil
4 pitta breads
1 head of lettuce, shredded
salt and pepper

Yoghurt dip
70g fat-free Greek-style yoghurt
2 tbsp fresh parsley, finely chopped
juice of ½ lemon

1. Heat a pan over a medium heat, add the olive oil and gently fry the onion and garlic until softened.
2. In a large bowl combine the lamb and beef mince, spices, oregano, tomato purée and lemon zest. Mix well and season with salt and pepper.
3. Add the onion mixture, combine well and place in the fridge for a few hours.
4. Soak the wooden skewers in water for 15 minutes.
5. Divide the meat mixture into eight equal pieces. Gently squeeze the meat around the skewers to form log-shaped kebabs, spreading the meat to an even thickness.

6. Chill the kebabs in the fridge until you're ready to grill.
7. To make the yoghurt dip, combine the ingredients in a serving bowl.
8. Preheat the grill, griddle pan or barbecue.
9. Spray the kebabs with cooking oil and cook for 8–10 minutes, turning occasionally, until golden brown and fully cooked through.
10. Add the pittas to the grill and heat through.
11. Slip the kebabs off the skewers into the pittas, adding some lettuce and 1 tablespoon of yoghurt dip to each. Serve immediately.

Serves 4 | **Nutrition** | 404 calories | 35g protein | 33g carbs | 14g fat

BARBECUE CHICKEN CALZONE

Ahhh, the folded, stuffed-with-mouth-watering-gooey cheesy centre pizza magic. Does life get any better than this? Once you've mastered this you'll most likely be making it every weekend – you've been warned.

The dough requires only a few ingredients, and you can use the same dough for home-made pizzas. Stuff it with your favourite toppings, bake until crisp and golden, and then get stuck in!

For a vegetarian version, swap the chicken for your favourite high protein meat alternative.

150g cooked chicken, shredded

2 tbsp barbecue sauce

170g self-raising flour

70g fat-free Greek-style yoghurt

1 tsp garlic powder

1 tbsp pizza sauce

60g light mozzarella, chopped into chunks

1 egg, beaten

1 tbsp dried oregano

200g crunchy salad (see Sides, page 209)

1. Preheat the oven to 220°C/200°C fan/gas 7.

2. Mix together the chicken and barbecue sauce.

3. In a bowl, combine the flour, yoghurt and garlic powder and mix well to form a dough.

4. Roll out the dough into a 25cm diameter circle, then add the pizza sauce to one side of the dough.

5. Add half the mozzarella on top of the sauce, then add the chicken, then the remaining mozzarella.

6. Fold the other side of the dough over, then seal the edges by pressing with a fork.

7. Brush with the beaten egg, sprinkle with oregano and bake for 18 minutes until golden brown and crispy.

8. Serve with a crunchy salad.

Serves 2 | **Nutrition** | 569 calories | 43g protein | 77g carbs | 8g fat

PIZZA TOPPINGS and FILLINGS

CREATE YOUR OWN

I love to get creative, so experiment and have some fun with your toppings. I like a bit of spice, so a natural go-to is chilli sauce or dried chilli flakes on a pizza. But equally mushrooms, pesto, barbecue sauce – there are endless options. I'm not going to open the 'pineapple on a pizza' debate – that will divide the crowd!

HIDDEN VEGGIES

If cooking for little ones, who perhaps don't always love their veg, you'll rarely get many complaints when you say they're having pizza. Little do they know: pizza can be a great way to get them to eat more of the good stuff. The onions, the peppers, you name it, fire it on and they'll gulp it down. If you want to be sneaky, grate the veg so it's hardly noticeable.

CRISPY, CRUNCHY TOPPINGS

For an extra-crispy pizza, have a go at frying the base in a pan. This will give you that bit more crunch; it works really well with thin pizzas.

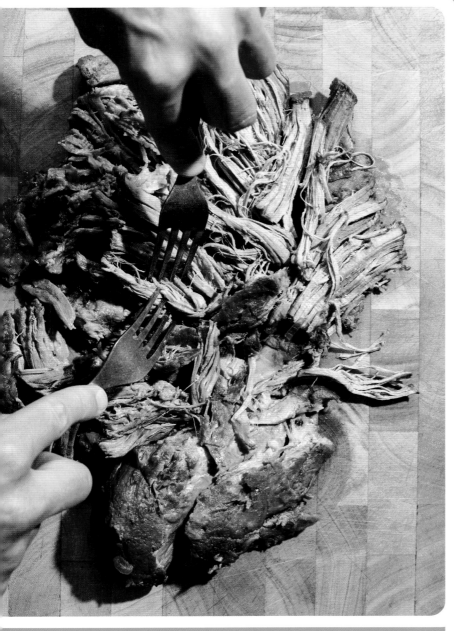

AIR FRYER *and* SLOW COOKER

AF STICKY SALMON

Salmon in the air fryer? And sticky salmon at that. This is one of the easiest recipes in the book, yet some marinated, beautifully cooked salmon will always have the family looking for more.

This one is perfect for those days when you've done long hours at work and need to whip up something that's tasty, healthy and aligned with your calorie and protein goals. It's also very versatile, so feel free to play around with different marinade combinations.

1 tbsp honey

1 tbsp garlic purée

3 tbsp light soy sauce

2 skinless salmon fillets, about 130g each

300g mashed potatoes (see Sides, page 210)

160g steamed fine green beans

Low calorie switch:
crunchy salad

1. In a dish, combine the honey, garlic and soy sauce. Add the salmon and marinate for 20 minutes.

2. Cook in the air fryer at 180°C for 10 minutes.

3. Serve with some fluffy mash and fine green beans.

TIP: I like to make double the salmon portion and use the leftover for sandwiches for the next few days.

Serves 2

Nutrition | 436 calories | 32g protein | 37g carbs | 16.5g fat

AF

CRISPY HONEY CHICKEN BURGER

That's four words that go well together. If you were to imagine your ideal chicken burger, this isn't far off what you'd be after, is it? Cook this for your friends and they will not believe that you have done it from scratch. You might want to save it for the neighbourhood barbecue and casually pop these out; you'll be the talk o' the toon!

2 skinless chicken breasts, about 150g each

1 tsp garlic powder

1 tsp onion salt

1 tsp smoked paprika

1 egg, beaten

40g corn chips (I use Flamin' Hot Doritos), crushed

2 brioche buns, lightly toasted

60g light coleslaw

200g crunchy salad (see Sides, page 209)

Sauce

30g honey

2 tbsp light soy sauce

1 tsp chipotle paste

1 tsp white wine vinegar

Low calorie switch:

sandwich thin, low calorie wrap or thin bagel

1. Place the chicken on a chopping board and use a small sharp knife to slice into it from the thicker side, ensuring you don't cut all the way through so you can open it out like a book. Cover with clingfilm, then gently bash with a rolling pin to make thin, even slices.

2. Season the chicken with garlic powder, onion salt and smoked paprika.

3. Dip the flattened chicken in the beaten egg, allow any excess egg to drip off and then coat in the crushed corn chips.

4. Cook in the air fryer at 180°C for 20 minutes.

5. Meanwhile, make the sauce: put the honey, soy sauce, chipotle paste, vinegar and 100ml water into a pan over a medium heat and stir until thickened.

6. Once the chicken is cooked, place on a lightly toasted brioche bun and top with the sauce and coleslaw.

7. Serve with a crunchy salad.

Serves 2 | **Nutrition** | 589 calories | 49g protein | 60g carbs | 14.1g fat

AF NO BREAD TOASTIE

Don't get me wrong, I love bread. However, imagine that chicken is bread…I need you to just go with this one. It's bold, unconventional and, dare I say it, wild! Layer up those breaded crispy chicken slices with ham, melted cheese and pickle and you have one of the finest creations you'll ever taste.

This one is designed to be flexible and I've tried it with a tablespoon of condensed mushroom soup in between – utterly gorgeous. It packs a bucketload of protein too, so should help keep those hunger cravings at bay.

2 skinless chicken breasts, about 150g each

40g plain flour

60ml egg whites

70g panko breadcrumbs

1 tbsp garlic powder

1 tbsp smoked paprika

10–12 sprays light cooking oil

4 large slices of ham

40g light mature Cheddar, grated

2 tbsp pickle or chutney

20g Red Leicester, grated

210g rainbow salad (see Sides, page 209)

1. Place clingfilm over the chicken breasts and pound with a mallet or rolling pin until the chicken is 2cm thick, then cut each breast in half.

2. Set out three dishes: one with the flour, one with the egg whites and one with the breadcrumbs combined with the garlic powder and smoked paprika.

3. Coat each piece of chicken in the flour, then in the egg whites, allowing any excess egg to drip off, and then press firmly into the breadcrumb mixture.

4. Place in the air fryer and spray with light cooking oil. Cook at 190°C for 14 minutes, turning after 7 minutes.

5. Once the chicken is cooked, add the ham, Cheddar and pickle to two pieces of chicken, then place the other pieces of chicken on top, with the Red Leicester on top of that.

6. Cook in the air fryer for 3–4 minutes until the cheese has melted.

7. Serve with rainbow salad.

Serves 2 | **Nutrition** | 530 calories | 58g protein | 49g carbs | 10.6g fat

AF

CHEESY CHICKEN SAUSAGE ROLLS

Oh hello! How good does this recipe look? I absolutely love sausage rolls, but sausage rolls that are healthy and packed with protein beat the high-street options for me. These are really easy to make and work out perfectly in the air fryer.

I'd have two of these for lunch, maybe with a mixed salad. They're also ideal for packed lunches or picnics. I find they go down very well if you're having people round and putting out a wee spread.

320g ready-rolled puff pastry

500g chicken mince

100g panko breadcrumbs

1 garlic clove, finely chopped

1 tbsp smoked paprika

2 tbsp barbecue sauce

1 tsp olive oil

100g light Cheddar, grated

1 egg, plus 1 egg, beaten

1 tbsp sesame seeds

salt and pepper

105g rainbow salad per person (see Sides, page 209)

1. Remove the puff pastry from the fridge.

2. In a large bowl, combine the chicken mince, breadcrumbs, garlic, smoked paprika, barbecue sauce, olive oil, cheese, salt, pepper and one egg.

3. Cut the pastry in half and roll out to make two A4-sized (30 x 21cm) rectangles.

4. Shape the mince mixture into two long sausage shapes and place along the centre of each piece of pastry.

5. Brush the sides with beaten egg. Carefully fold the pastry over to create two long sausage rolls. Press down on the edges with a fork to seal.

6. Cut each half into four equal sausage rolls.

7. Brush the tops with the beaten egg and sprinkle with sesame seeds.

8. Place the sausage rolls in the air fryer and cook at 190°C for 14 minutes until golden brown.

9. Serve immediately, with rainbow salad.

Makes 8
sausage rolls

Nutrition | 390 calories | 23g protein | 35g carbs | 16.8g fat
(1 roll)

SMOKY CHIPOTLE HONEY CHICKEN TENDERS

Guys, you will love this. Kids, adults, dogs, grumpy next-door neighbour, everyone will love these chicken tenders.

Nothing complex about the cooking of them either. Basically, once you have the sauce sorted and a plan for your sides, the rest of the work is done by the ole babe magnet, aka the air fryer.

The chicken tenders are very versatile. I like slicing them up and making them the base of a sandwich or wrap or, as suggested here, serving alongside a creamy potato salad. Get stuck into these, thank me later.

300g skinless chicken breast, cut into strips
3 tbsp barbecue seasoning (I use Schwartz)
2 tbsp smoked paprika
80ml egg whites
70g cornflakes, finely crushed
250g potato salad (see Sides, page 210)

Sauce
100g smoky chipotle barbecue sauce
1 tbsp chipotle paste
1 tbsp Worcestershire sauce
2 tbsp tomato ketchup
1 tbsp honey

1. Place the chicken strips in a large bowl and combine with the barbecue seasoning and smoked paprika.
2. Dip each chicken strip into the egg whites, then allow any excess egg to drip off before pressing firmly into the cornflakes.
3. Cook in the air fryer at 190°C for 17 minutes, turning after 9 minutes.

4. For the sauce, mix all the ingredients together in a bowl.
5. Once the chicken is cooked, dip the strips in the sauce until fully coated.
6. Serve alongside potato salad.

Serves 2

Nutrition | 570 calories | 51g protein | 85g carbs | 3.5g fat

AF

GLAZED HAM JOINT

This is a go-to for a Sunday roast. Get the whole family round the table, bash out a few sides and bang, you have your main attraction for the perfect Sunday meal. Not a lot of ingredients here, and it's nice and easy. You just need to take a little care with the timings and painting on the glaze while the ham is roasting.

I would suggest using the time between paintings to put together your sides. I like some asparagus or broccoli, glazed carrots, sweet potato and mash, but the possibilities are endless.

3 tbsp zero calorie brown sugar alternative (I use Pure Via)

3 tbsp honey

2 tbsp marmalade

1 tbsp wholegrain mustard

½ an orange

900g ham joint

mashed potatoes (150g per person, see Sides, page 210)

steamed broccoli (100g per person)

1. Combine the brown sugar, honey, marmalade and mustard in a bowl and mix well.

2. Squeeze in the juice of half an orange and stir well.

3. Put the ham joint on a doubled sheet of foil. Coat the ham joint all over with half the honey mixture and double wrap the joint in the foil.

4. Cook in the air fryer at 170°C for 25 minutes.

5. Remove the ham from the air fryer and paint it with most of the remaining honey mixture, reserving a little for the final glazing.

6. Pop the ham back into the air fryer for a further 15 minutes at 170°C.

7. Remove the ham from the air fryer and remove the foil.

8. Paint the joint all over with the remaining honey mixture and put it back into the air fryer at 190°C for 7 minutes.

9. Leave the joint to rest for 5–10 minutes before carving.

10. Serve with mash and broccoli.

Serves 9 slices (100g each)

Nutrition | 413 calories | 36g protein | 53g carbs | 7.2g fat

AF CHICKEN PARM

Who doesn't love a chicken parm? It is without doubt one of my favourites. This is a punchier one in terms of calories, and also has that wee splash of red wine in it, so maybe this is the meal for a celebration, or a little kick-start to the weekend.

A healthy 49 grams of protein with each serving, keeping you fuelled throughout the evening, and ensuring you hit your macro targets.

2 skinless chicken breasts, about 150g each
2 tbsp plain flour
60ml egg whites
50g dried breadcrumbs
50g Parmesan, grated
1 tbsp garlic salt
70g light mature Cheddar, grated
salt and pepper
210g rainbow salad (see Sides, page 209)

Sauce
1 tsp light butter
1 onion, finely sliced
3 garlic cloves, finely chopped
1 x 400g tin chopped tomatoes
1 tbsp dried oregano
70ml red wine

1. Place the chicken on a chopping board and use a small sharp knife to slice into it from the thicker side, ensuring you don't cut all the way through so you can open it out like a book. Cover with clingfilm, then gently bash with a rolling pin to make thin, even slices.

2. Season with salt and pepper, then set out three dishes: one with the flour, one with the egg whites and one with the breadcrumbs combined with the Parmesan and garlic salt.

3. Coat each piece of chicken in the flour, then in the egg whites, allowing any excess egg to drip off. Finally coat well with the breadcrumb mixture.

4. Cook the chicken in the air fryer at 180°C for 14 minutes.

5. Meanwhile, make the sauce: melt the butter in a pan, add the onion and cook until softened.

6. Add the garlic, tomatoes, oregano and red wine and cook for a few minutes until the mixture thickens slightly.

7. Once the chicken is cooked, pour the sauce on top and scatter over the grated cheese.

8. Air fry at 180°C for 3–4 minutes or until the cheese has melted.

9. Serve with rainbow salad.

Serves 2 | **Nutrition** | 596 calories | 49g protein | 48g carbs | 14g fat

SWEET *and* SOUR CHICKEN

Just like our favourite local takeaway. That's some of the feedback I've had on this one: people think it's just as good as the experts'. This recipe is packed with 40 grams of protein per serving, it isn't too difficult and it's bursting with flavour – wait until that tangy goodness hits your taste buds ... yummy!

600g skinless chicken breast, cut into chunks

1 tbsp sesame oil

2 tbsp dark soy sauce

1 tsp finely chopped or grated garlic

1 tsp finely chopped or grated ginger

80g cornflour

4 tbsp tomato ketchup

1 tbsp malt vinegar

2 tbsp honey

2 tbsp zero calorie brown sugar alternative (I use Pure Via)

6 slices tinned pineapple, cut into chunks, plus half the juice from the tin

8–10 sprays light olive oil

1 onion, finely diced

1 red or green pepper, diced

2 packets microwave basmati rice (500g cooked weight)

Low calorie switch:
konjac rice or cauliflower rice

1. Put the chicken into a large bowl and combine with the sesame oil, dark soy, garlic and ginger.

2. Add the cornflour and mix well until all the chicken is coated.

3. Cook in the air fryer at 200°C for 17 minutes.

4. Meanwhile, in a bowl combine the tomato ketchup, malt vinegar, honey, brown sugar and the pineapple juice, to make the sauce.

5. Heat a pan over a medium heat and spray with olive oil. Add the onion and cook for about 4 minutes until softened. Add the pepper and cook for a further 3 minutes.

6. Add the sauce, pineapple chunks and cooked chicken. Mix well and serve with basmati rice.

Serves 4

Nutrition | 535 calories | 40g protein | 79g carbs | 7g fat

AF

SALT *and* PEPPER CHICKEN

This is a real people pleaser and I love to make it midweek as it feels like such a fakeaway treat. Once you've whipped this one up, you'll no longer be ordering food from your phone. Could save you a fortune too!

As a timesaver, why don't you chop up and marinate the chicken overnight in the fridge? You can also prepare the spice mix in advance, so that when you come to cook it, you've already done most of the work. All that's left to do is to pop the chicken in the babe magnet – you may know it as the air fryer – and bang, you've got another 10/10 meal.

600g boneless skinless chicken thighs, cut into chunks
2 tbsp white rice vinegar
2 tbsp sriracha sauce
1 tbsp dark soy sauce
1 tsp Chinese five spice
juice of 1 lime
1 tbsp garlic powder
60g cornflour
10–12 sprays light cooking oil
1 red chilli, finely sliced
2 spring onions, finely sliced
2 packets microwave basmati rice (500g cooked weight)

Spice mix
1 tsp chicken seasoning
½ tsp salt
1 tbsp ground white pepper
1 tsp Chinese five spice

1. Put the chicken in a large bowl with the rice vinegar, sriracha, soy sauce, five spice, lime juice, garlic powder and leave in the fridge to marinate for at least 15 minutes – or overnight.
2. Gently toss each piece of chicken in the cornflour until they're all fully coated.
3. Place in the air fryer and spray with light cooking oil. Cook at 190°C for 10 minutes, turning after 5 minutes.

4. Increase the heat to 200°C, then cook for a further 4–5 minutes or until golden brown.
5. Meanwhile, combine all the ingredients for the spice mix.
6. Remove from the air fryer and toss in the spice mix.
7. Garnish with sliced chilli and spring onions and serve immediately, with basmati rice.

Low calorie switch:
konjac rice or cauliflower rice

Serves 4

Nutrition | 563 calories | 40g protein | 52g carbs | 21g fat

TIP: This works really well in wraps as a lunch option.

AF SRIRACHA TOFU RICE BOWL

If you are vegan, meat-free, or just trying to cut down on meat, good ole tofu is the golden choice. For this one, we're using extra firm tofu that we've pressed in advance. If, like me, you like your tofu crispy, give it slightly longer in the air fryer for extra crunch. With 40 grams of protein for a meat-free dish, this is a huge win!

I like my food spicy, so I'm happy to be extra liberal with the sriracha, whereas others might prefer to cut it down. Either way, this will look and taste fantastic.

400g extra firm tofu
3 tbsp sriracha sauce
2 garlic cloves, finely chopped
1 tbsp light soy sauce
1 tbsp light sweet chilli sauce
20 sprays light cooking oil
1 packet basmati microwave rice (250g cooked weight)
150g edamame beans, boiled or microwaved
2 spring onions, finely chopped
salt and pepper

Low calorie switch:
konjac rice or cauliflower rice

1. Start at least 24 hours in advance by pressing the tofu to remove excess water.
2. The next day, cut the tofu into cubes and place in a mixing bowl with the sriracha sauce, garlic, soy sauce, sweet chilli sauce, salt and pepper. Mix until the tofu is fully coated.
3. Spray the base of the air fryer with cooking oil, then add the tofu and cook at 200°C for 10–12 minutes.

4. Microwave the rice and combine it with the warm edamame beans.
5. Stir in the tofu, then garnish with spring onions.

Serves 2 | **Nutrition** | 597 calories | 40g protein | 51g carbs | 24.5g fat

AF

DONER KEBABS

It's not often we think of kebab coming in at less than 600 calories. I'm sure when I used to stumble out of the pub it had more calories than that. This'll have the additional benefit of saving you a little coin as well. Winner-winner, doner-dinner – what do you think, will that catch on? To be honest, the chilli sauce alone here should win some sort of award.

You'll need to mix up the mince and leave it to marinate overnight. You could also prep the sauce the day before and keep it in the fridge. Serve on some high protein flatbreads, add salad and sauce, then put it right in your face. Delish!

400g lean lamb mince (10% fat)

1 egg

1 tsp olive oil

1 tbsp garlic powder

1 tbsp chilli powder

1 tsp ground coriander

1 tsp ground cumin

1 tsp paprika

salt and pepper

Sauce

1 x 400g tin chopped tomatoes

1 garlic clove, finely chopped

2 hot chillies, finely chopped

1 tsp cayenne pepper

1 tbsp zero calorie brown sugar
  alternative (I use Pure Via)

1 tbsp olive oil

1 tbsp apple cider vinegar

To serve

4 high protein flatbreads
  (I use Deli Kitchen Carb
  Lite Wraps), warmed

½ red onion, sliced

¼ cucumber, cut into chunks

4 tomatoes, cut into chunks

½ head of lettuce, shredded

Low calorie switch:

sandwich thin

1. Place the lamb, egg, olive oil and all the spices, salt and pepper in a large bowl, mix well and leave in the fridge to marinate overnight.

2. The next day, tip into a food processor and blitz to form a paste.

3. Shape into a large cylinder, then tightly wrap in foil.

4. Cook in the air fryer at 170°C for 40 minutes, then remove the foil and cook for a further 10 minutes.

5. Meanwhile, make the sauce by blitzing all the ingredients in a blender until smooth.

6. Cut the meat in thin slices, using the blade of a grater or a long, thin, sharp knife.

7. Serve on warm flatbreads with the vegetables and chilli sauce.

Serves 4 | **Nutrition** | 577 calories | 32g protein | 55g carbs | 27g fat

AF STICKY HONEY MEATBALLS

If you've not made meatballs in the babe magnet yet, what are you waiting for? They're golden and crispy on the outside and gorgeously moist inside. Pair with a sticky honey garlic sauce and you've got yourself a marriage made in heaven.

If you want more sauce ideas I'd recommend the Chicken Parm sauce (page 155).

500g lean beef mince (5% fat)
1 onion, finely chopped
60g panko breadcrumbs
1 tbsp garlic powder
1 egg, beaten
1 tsp olive oil
10–12 sprays light cooking oil
1 tsp sesame seeds
2 spring onions, finely chopped
salt and pepper
2 packets microwave jasmine rice
   (500g cooked weight)

Sauce

4 tbsp rice vinegar
2 tbsp zero calorie brown sugar
   alternative (I use Pure Via)
4 tbsp light soy sauce
2 tbsp honey
3 garlic cloves, finely chopped
1 tsp cornflour

1. In a large bowl, combine the mince, onion, breadcrumbs, garlic powder, egg, olive oil, salt and pepper and mix well.
2. Using your hands, roll the mixture into 25–30 meatballs.
3. Place in the air fryer and spray with light cooking oil. Cook at 190°C for 14 minutes, turning every 3–4 minutes.
4. Meanwhile, make the sauce: put all the ingredients in a bowl, add 3 tablespoons of water and whisk well.

5. Place a pan over a medium heat, add the sauce and cook for 3–4 minutes until the mixture becomes sticky and slightly thicker.
6. Add the meatballs to the sauce and stir to coat.
7. Scatter over the sesame seeds and spring onions and serve with jasmine rice.

Serves 4 | **Nutrition** | 468 calories | 40g protein | 50g carbs | 11.7g fat

SC SALMON CURRY

A lot of my favourite meals have salmon as the main ingredient. For this mild, coconutty curry, I prefer to use skinless salmon fillets, so then it's just a case of compiling the ingredients and letting the slow cooker do all the work for you.

This is a great one to make on a weekend afternoon. Pop it on and it'll be ready to be devoured for a really special dinner that night.

1 x 400ml tin light coconut milk

1 x 400g tin chopped tomatoes

3 tbsp tomato purée

150ml boiling vegetable stock

1 tbsp ground cumin

1 tbsp chilli powder

1 tsp turmeric

1 tbsp smoked paprika

4 large skinless salmon fillets, about 130g each

1 onion, chopped

3 carrots, peeled and chopped into chunks

4 garlic cloves, chopped

2 tbsp finely chopped fresh root ginger

2 tbsp finely chopped fresh parsley

salt and pepper

2 packets roasted vegetable couscous (200g)

Low calorie switch:

konjac rice or cauliflower rice

1. Put the coconut milk, chopped tomatoes, tomato purée, vegetable stock, spices, salt and pepper into the slow cooker and mix well.

2. Add the salmon, onion, carrots, garlic and ginger.

3. Put the lid on and cook on low for 2½ hours.

4. Garnish with parsley and serve with fluffy vegetable couscous.

TIP: Don't worry if it gets messy — the rules are the chef doesn't wash up!

Serves 4 | **Nutrition** | 521 calories | 36g protein | 46g carbs | 21g fat

SC

CHILLI CHICKEN CURRY

This is a masterpiece of flavours. The aroma of the finished dish will have the family running into the kitchen, and they'll be looking for seconds. They might even offer to wash up, but no guarantees there.

There is not much work here other than the initial prep, and that's just as it should be with a slow cooker, freeing you up while the meal is cooking.

I've opted for pilau rice, but choose a different rice for a new twist on the meal.

600g skinless chicken breast, diced

1 tbsp olive oil

1 onion, finely chopped

3 garlic cloves, finely chopped

2cm fresh root ginger, peeled and grated

1 x 400g tin chopped tomatoes

2 tbsp tomato purée

1 cinnamon stick

4 cloves

1 tbsp chilli powder

2 tbsp garam masala

1 tsp turmeric

4 cardamom pods

100ml light coconut milk

handful of fresh coriander, roughly chopped

2 packets pilau basmati microwave rice (500g cooked weight)

Low calorie switch:
konjac rice or cauliflower rice

1. Put the chicken in the slow cooker and add the oil, onion, garlic, ginger, chopped tomatoes, tomato purée and all the spices.

2. Put the lid on and cook on high for 3 hours or low for 5 hours.

3. Stir in the coconut milk and cook for a further 45 minutes.

4. Sprinkle with coriander and serve with pilau rice.

TIP: A great one to double up the recipe and freeze the rest.

Serves 4

Nutrition | 447 calories | 42g protein | 44g carbs | 7.7g fat

SC PEANUT CHICKEN

Similar to a chicken satay, this takes me back to my time travelling in Southeast Asia, which is really where my love of food started. There are quite a few ingredients here, but believe me when I say the combination is inspired! This is where the slow cooker really comes into its own, blending everything together wonderfully. Ideal for when you're going to be entertaining in the evening.

With a healthy 36 grams of protein for 503 calories, this is a great one for anyone who is training.

600g skinless chicken breast, cut into chunks
juice of 1 lime
2 tbsp rice vinegar
4 tbsp light soy sauce
2 tbsp light sweet chilli sauce
1 tbsp fish sauce
2 garlic cloves, finely chopped
2 tbsp grated fresh root ginger
1 tbsp chilli powder
2 tbsp zero calorie brown sugar alternative (I use Pure Via)
250ml chicken stock
1 x 400ml tin light coconut milk
3 tbsp peanut butter
2 tbsp fresh parsley, roughly chopped
600g mashed potatoes (see Sides, page 210)
400g steamed broccoli

Low calorie switch:
crunchy salad

1. Put the chicken in a bowl with the lime juice, rice vinegar, soy sauce, sweet chilli sauce, fish sauce, garlic, ginger, chilli powder and brown sugar and marinate for at least 15 minutes.
2. Put the chicken and its marinade into the slow cooker, then add the stock, coconut milk and peanut butter and mix well.
3. Put the lid on and cook on low for 6 hours or high for 4 hours.
4. Garnish with parsley and serve alongside fluffy mash and broccoli.

Serves 4 | **Nutrition** | 503 calories | 36g protein | 41g carbs | 17.5g fat

SC PULLED PORK

This is one we all fancy when we're out at a restaurant, but master it at home and you can have it any time you want. Incredibly easy to put together and one to look forward to all day.

When fully cooked, the pork should separate easily with a fork, and you can spread it across bread or a bun for an unrivalled pulled-pork sandwich. I'm a massive fan of combining this with mash tatties and broccoli for the ultimate well balanced meal. This is ideal if you're having the neighbours round, or if the little one has friends visiting.

1 onion, finely diced

6 tbsp tomato ketchup

3 tbsp sriracha sauce

4 tbsp apple cider vinegar

3 tbsp tomato purée

1 tbsp garlic powder

1 tbsp paprika

1 tsp mustard powder

1 tsp ground cumin

1.5kg pork shoulder, trimmed of
    excess fat (trimmed weight 1.25kg)

salt and pepper

mashed potatoes (150g per person,
    see Sides, page 210)

800g steamed broccoli

Low calorie switch:
crunchy salad

1. Combine all the ingredients, except the pork, in a bowl and stir well.

2. Put the pork into the slow cooker and season with salt and pepper.

3. Cover with the sauce, then put the lid on and cook on low for 7–8 hours.

4. Pull the pork into shreds using two forks. Serve with mash and broccoli.

TIP: Pulled pork is one of the most versatile options — it goes great in burgers, wraps, salad, with veg, you name it!

Serves 8 | **Nutrition** | 447 calories | 45g protein | 34g carbs | 15g fat

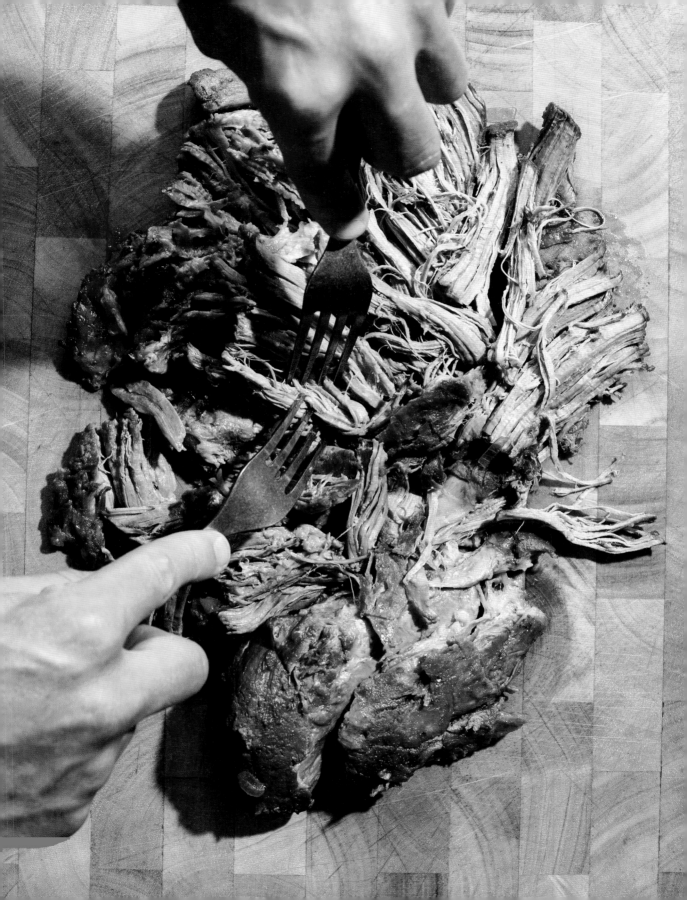

SC SPICY BEEF

This is definitely one for when you are trying to impress. It needs to be marinated overnight, so planning ahead is important.

Get that marinade bashed together and you have yourself a feast in the making. It does have a little kick so perhaps this is more of a meal for the adults than the kids.

Really easy to prep this spicy beef ahead and throw it together with rice or sweet potatoes, and you have your lunches for the week sorted.

500g lean beef, visible fat removed, cut into bite-sized pieces
5 tbsp fat-free Greek-style yoghurt
2 tbsp mild curry powder
½ tsp salt
1 onion, finely sliced
3 garlic cloves, crushed
2cm fresh root ginger, peeled and grated
2 chillies, finely sliced
1 bay leaf
1 cinnamon stick
3 cloves
4 green cardamom pods, bruised
200g passata
200ml hot beef stock
chopped fresh coriander
2 packets microwave basmati rice (500g cooked weight)

1. Put the beef in a small bowl with the yoghurt, curry powder and salt. Stir to mix, then cover with clingfilm and leave to marinate in the fridge overnight.

2. Add the marinated beef mixture to the slow cooker with the onion, garlic, ginger, chillies, bay leaf, spices and passata. Pour over the beef stock and stir well.

3. Put the lid on and cook on low for 7–8 hours or until the meat is melt-in-the-mouth tender.

4. Taste for seasoning, then sprinkle with chopped coriander and serve with basmati rice.

Serves 4

Nutrition | 418 calories | 34g protein | 45g carbs | 10g fat

SC LAMB STEW

This is a perfect hearty-but-healthy weekend dinner or Sunday lunch special. You can pop it all in the slow cooker on low overnight and it melts in your mouth the next day.

It won't eat into your relaxing time as it's so quick and easy to prepare, and then you just leave it alone and let the slow cooker work its magic.

Packing a tremendous 62 grams of protein per serving, as well as lots of healthy vegetables, this dish is guaranteed to satisfy any appetite.

2 tbsp light butter

600g boneless lamb shoulder, cut into chunks

1 onion, roughly chopped

1 tbsp tomato purée

2 carrots, peeled and cut into chunks

800g potatoes, chopped

300ml boiling beef stock

1 tbsp Worcestershire sauce

2 bay leaves

2 fresh rosemary sprigs

2 fresh thyme sprigs

80g frozen peas

4 slices crusty tiger bread

Low calorie switch:

sandwich thin or lower calorie bread

1. Heat 1 tablespoon of the butter in a pan over a high heat, add the lamb and cook for 3 minutes until evenly browned. Transfer to the slow cooker.

2. Add the remaining butter to the pan and gently fry the onion until softened. Add the tomato purée and stir for 1 minute, then add the mixture to the slow cooker.

3. Add the carrots, potatoes, beef stock, Worcestershire sauce, bay leaves, rosemary and thyme to the slow cooker.

4. Put the lid on and cook on low for 8 hours until the lamb is tender.

5. Add the peas and cook for a further 10 minutes.

6. Serve immediately with crusty tiger bread.

Serves 4

Nutrition | 598 calories | 62g protein | 65g carbs | 12g fat

MEAL PREP

CHICKEN SAUSAGE PASTA

This is a top fan favourite. Chicken sausages are one of the greatest inventions of modern times, and I love popping them in my meal prep recipes. They deliver well on the protein front too, giving 34 grams in each serving of this dish.

Combining the flavours of tomatoes, soft cheese and garlic with pasta is a real winner for meal prep. Given that it's very easy to throw together, for me this is a midweek option. You know when you're tired but you still want to treat yourself? Yeah, this is the meal for that time.

280g rigatoni

10 chicken sausages

8–10 sprays light cooking oil

3–4 shallots, finely chopped

4 garlic cloves, finely chopped

200g baby tomatoes, chopped

large handful of spinach, shredded

50g sun-dried tomatoes, chopped

150g light soft cheese

2 chicken stock cubes

125g light mozzarella, chopped into chunks

salt and pepper

handful of fresh coriander, finely chopped

1. Bring a large pan of salted water to the boil and put the rigatoni in to cook until al dente.

2. Preheat the grill to medium. Grill the chicken sausages for 10–12 minutes until cooked through.

3. Heat a large frying pan over a medium heat and spray with the cooking oil, then add the shallot and cook until softened.

4. Add the garlic and the baby tomatoes and cook for 2 minutes.

5. Add the spinach, sun-dried tomatoes and soft cheese, stirring continuously.

6. Crumble the stock cubes into the mix, then add a ladleful of the pasta cooking water to create a sauce consistency.

7. Once your chicken sausages are cooked, chop them into bite-sized chunks and add to the pan.

8. Drain the pasta and then add to the pan.

9. Add the mozzarella and mix in until it melts.

10. Divide into four equal portions, add to meal prep containers and that's you sorted. To serve, sprinkle with coriander.

Serves 4 | **Nutrition** | 510 calories | 34g protein | 64g carbs | 14g fat

CREAMY CAJUN CHICKEN PASTA

Pretty straightforward to cook, and the Cajun seasoning really brings this recipe to life. It's under 500 calories, so it works well if you're watching your intake. For a vegetarian version, swap the chicken for your favourite meat-free alternative and use vegetable stock.

This works just as well with rice or noodles if you're looking for a bit of variety.

250g penne pasta

600g skinless chicken breast, cut into chunks

4 tbsp Cajun seasoning (I use Schwartz)

2 tbsp smoked paprika

10–12 sprays light cooking oil

1 onion, finely diced

2 red peppers, thinly sliced

2 garlic cloves, finely chopped

3 tbsp tomato purée

80g light soft cheese

2 tbsp fat-free Greek-style yoghurt

130ml boiling chicken stock

1 tbsp chilli flakes

handful of fresh coriander, roughly chopped

1. Bring a large pan of salted water to the boil and put the pasta in to cook until al dente.

2. Put the chicken in a large bowl with half the Cajun seasoning and half the smoked paprika and toss until coated.

3. Heat a large frying pan over a medium heat and spray with cooking oil. Add the chicken and fry for 10 minutes until golden brown.

4. Add the onion, peppers, garlic, the remaining Cajun seasoning and paprika and cook for another 3 minutes.

5. Add the tomato purée, soft cheese, yoghurt and chicken stock to create a sauce consistency.

6. Drain the pasta, add to the sauce mixture and stir well.

7. Divide into four equal portions and add to meal prep containers. Serve scattered with chilli flakes and coriander.

Serves 4

Nutrition | 493 calories | 47g protein | 46g carbs | 15g fat

CHICKEN and CHORIZO RIGATONI

This has been one of the most successful recipes in the meal prep category – people seem to love it. It delivers an amazing 51 grams of protein per serving and will well and truly deal with those hunger cravings. I love to tuck into the big chunky rigatoni pasta, complemented by the combination of chorizo with sun-dried tomatoes and some cream – 'get in ma belly'. It's quick, simple to make and always delicious.

8–10 sprays light cooking oil

600g skinless chicken breast, chopped into chunks

1 tsp smoked paprika

1 onion, finely chopped

60g chorizo, diced

240g rigatoni

2 tbsp tomato purée

60g sun-dried tomatoes, chopped

4 tbsp single cream

large handful of spinach, shredded

1 tbsp grated Parmesan

salt and pepper

1. Heat a large frying pan over a medium heat and spray with cooking oil. Add the chicken, smoked paprika, salt and pepper and brown for 8 minutes.

2. Add the onion and chorizo and cook for a further 4 minutes.

3. Bring a large pan of salted water to the boil and put the rigatoni in to cook until al dente.

4. Add the tomato purée, sun-dried tomatoes and cream to the chicken mixture.

5. Pour in a ladleful of the pasta cooking water to create a sauce consistency.

6. Drain the pasta and add it to the pan with the chicken.

7. Stir in the spinach and scatter the Parmesan across the mixture.

8. Divide into four equal portions and add to meal prep containers.

Serves 4 | **Nutrition** | 514 calories | 51g protein | 49g carbs | 12g fat

CARBONARA ORZO

I honestly love pasta. I'm sure you've guessed that from the number of recipes in which I use pasta, and orzo is one of the best: the texture is just amazing. If you want it softer, cook it for a little longer than the packet says, but for me I'm going al dente.

This recipe packs a big creamy velvety punch and will give you four delightful lunches or dinners. Packing a whopping 60 grams of protein for 558 calories means it is a great choice for any diet.

8–10 sprays light cooking oil
1 red onion, chopped
600g skinless chicken breast, cut
  into bite-sized chunks
2 tsp onion salt
2 tsp dried oregano
4 unsmoked bacon medallions,
  chopped into cubes
200g mushrooms, sliced
240g orzo
700ml boiling chicken stock
  (2 stock cubes)
125g light soft cheese
60g Parmesan, finely grated
salt and pepper
handful of fresh parsley, chopped

1. Heat a large frying pan over a medium heat and spray with cooking oil. Add the onion and cook for 3–4 minutes until softened.
2. Season the chicken with salt, pepper, 1 teaspoon of the onion salt and 1 teaspoon of oregano. Add to the pan and brown for 7–8 minutes.
3. Add the bacon and cook for another few minutes.
4. Stir in the mushrooms and the remaining oregano and onion salt.

5. Mix in the orzo and gradually add the chicken stock. Bring to the boil and simmer over a low heat until the orzo has absorbed the stock and is al dente.
6. Stir in the soft cheese, then scatter the Parmesan on top.
7. Divide into four equal portions and add to meal prep containers. Serve scattered with parsley.

Serves 4 | **Nutrition** | 558 calories | 60g protein | 51g carbs | 11g fat

CREAMY GARLIC CHICKEN *and* CHORIZO ORZO

This is a great option whether you're cooking for the family or prepping for your fridge or freezer, delivering a healthy 52 grams of protein per serving, not to be sniffed at.

I'm a big fan of Boursin cheese: it adds a delicious flavour to any recipe and this is no exception. Meal prep can often get a bad rep as people think that you might be sacrificing taste for the convenience of bulk cooking. Your task now is to find people who think that, let them taste this, and hey presto, you've won them over.

8–10 sprays light cooking oil

70g chorizo, diced

600g skinless chicken breast, cut into chunks

4 garlic cloves, finely chopped

1 tbsp smoked paprika

1 red onion, finely chopped

1 red pepper, diced

240g orzo

700ml boiling chicken stock

100g garlic and herbs cheese (I use Boursin)

salt and pepper

handful of fresh coriander, finely chopped

1. Heat a large frying pan over a medium heat and spray with cooking oil. Add the chorizo and fry until crispy. Remove the chorizo from the pan and set aside, leaving as much oil as possible in the pan.

2. Add the chicken to the pan and fry in the chorizo oil.

3. Add the garlic, smoked paprika, onion, red pepper, salt and pepper.

4. Mix in the orzo, followed by the chicken stock. Bring to the boil, then simmer for 15–20 minutes until the orzo is cooked.

5. Add the cheese and the cooked chorizo and mix well.

6. Divide into four equal portions and add to meal prep containers. Serve scattered with coriander.

TIP: The chorizo oil brings a lot of flavour to the chicken, so try not to lose any of it after crisping.

Serves 4 | **Nutrition** | 597 calories | 52g protein | 53g carbs | 19g fat

SALMON RISOTTO

If you know you're coming home to this from a hard day's graft, it'll keep you smiling. It's a great option for a midweek dinner and is a sound choice for your weekend meal prep.

The only thing you need to avoid is overcooking the risotto rice – keep testing it as you go and remove from the heat when it still has a little bite. No scoffing it though, or there will be none left for the dinner portions.

4 skinless salmon fillets, approx 130g each
1 tbsp light butter
1 onion, finely chopped
3 garlic cloves, finely chopped
240g risotto rice
200ml dry white wine
1.2 litres hot vegetable stock
2 lemons: 1 sliced, juice of 1
60g Parmesan, grated
200g medley of green veg (see Sides, page 211)
salt and pepper
handful of fresh parsley, roughly chopped

1. Preheat the oven to 210°C/190°C fan/gas 6½.

2. In a large pan over a medium heat, melt the butter, add the onion and garlic and cook for 3–4 minutes until softened.

3. Add the risotto rice and stir well, then add the wine. Allow the wine to reduce by half before adding the hot vegetable stock, a little at a time: the rice should absorb the stock before you add more.

4. Put the salmon fillets on a baking tray, season with salt and pepper and cover with slices of lemon. Squeeze on the juice of the other lemon and bake for 10 minutes. The salmon should not be fully cooked at this stage as it will continue to cook when added to the risotto. Flake the salmon.

5. When the risotto is almost cooked, but still has a little bite to it, add the salmon.

6. Stir in the Parmesan and the medley of cooked green vegetables.

7. Divide into four equal portions and add to meal prep containers. Serve garnished with parsley.

Serves 4

Nutrition | 580 calories | 38g protein | 56g carbs | 18g fat

CHICKEN *and* CHORIZO JAMBALAYA

Originally from Louisiana, USA, jambalaya is the queen of versatility. Switch out chicken for pork, beef, seafood or tofu; no matter what you choose, you will have a mouth-watering dish. Put your own twists on this by switching around the spices to create your very own taste sensation. The aroma this creates in the kitchen is irresistible, so don't be surprised if your neighbours pop round!

100g chorizo, cut into cubes

600g skinless chicken breast, cut into chunks

1 red onion, finely chopped

2 garlic cloves, crushed

1 green pepper, chopped

2 tbsp Cajun seasoning (I use Schwartz)

1 tbsp chilli powder

1 tbsp smoked paprika

300g white rice

1 litre boiling chicken stock

300g cherry tomatoes

salt and pepper

handful of basil, roughly chopped

1. Heat a large frying pan over a medium heat, add the chorizo and cook for about 3 minutes, until crispy. Remove from the pan, leaving as much oil in the pan as possible.

2. Add the chicken to the pan and cook for 6–7 minutes.

3. Add the onion, garlic and pepper and cook for about 5 minutes, until softened.

4. Add the Cajun seasoning, chilli powder, smoked paprika, salt and pepper and mix well. Once fully coated, add the rice and stir well for a minute.

5. Pour in the chicken stock and tomatoes, cover and simmer for 20 minutes until the rice is fully cooked through.

6. Stir in the cooked chorizo. Divide into four equal portions and add to meal prep containers. Serve scattered with basil.

Serves 4 | **Nutrition** | 570 calories | 52g protein | 66g carbs | 12g fat

PERI PERI GARLIC CHICKEN RICE

A cheeky take on a favourite chicken restaurant. You will most likely be familiar with the fantastic taste of peri peri, and with this recipe we're going to add our little twist. This is one of the lower calorie options in the book, so it's a great choice if you're monitoring your nutritional intake. Lots going on here flavour-wise and quite a lot of vegetables in this dish.

600g skinless chicken breast, cut into chunks

2 tsp cayenne pepper

2 tsp ground cumin

2 tbsp smoked paprika

2 tbsp dried oregano

1 tsp salt

1 tsp pepper

100ml garlic peri peri sauce

10–20 sprays light cooking oil

1 onion, finely diced

2 yellow peppers, cut into small chunks

3 garlic cloves, crushed

2 tbsp tomato purée

240g basmati rice

1 x 400g tin chopped tomatoes

400ml boiling chicken stock

salt and pepper

handful of fresh parsley, roughly chopped

1. Place the chicken in a large bowl, then combine it with 1 teaspoon of the cayenne pepper, 1 teaspoon of the cumin, 1 tablespoon of the smoked paprika, 1 tablespoon of the oregano, the salt and pepper and the garlic peri peri sauce.

2. Heat a large frying pan over a medium heat and lightly spray with cooking oil. Add the chicken and cook for 12 minutes, stirring occasionally, until fully cooked through. Remove the chicken from the pan and set to the side.

3. Spray some more oil into the pan, add the onion, peppers and garlic and cook for 3 minutes, then add the remaining spices.

4. Add the tomato purée and stir well, then add the rice, chopped tomatoes and chicken stock. Bring to the boil, then cover the pan and simmer until the rice is fully cooked through. Add a little extra rice if needed.

5. Mix the chicken into the rice mixture.

6. Divide into four equal portions and add to meal prep containers. Serve garnished with parsley.

Serves 4 | **Nutrition** | 474 calories | 46g protein | 62g carbs | 6g fat

STEAK and PEPPER STIR FRY

This really is a quick meal to prepare, and it works brilliantly either to eat immediately or as a meal prep choice. It could become the staple that you make time and time again and it hits those all-important macronutrient goals without compromising on taste.

You're making your own sauce, so you know exactly what you're eating. Suitable for all palates, but use less sriracha or leave it out altogether if you want a less spicy sauce.

10–12 sprays light cooking oil

1 red pepper, cut into 2cm squares

1 yellow pepper, cut into 2cm squares

600g flank steak, cut into strips

4 nests of fine egg noodles, cooked to the packet instructions

1 tbsp sesame seeds

Sauce

3 garlic cloves, finely chopped

3cm fresh root ginger, peeled and finely grated

5 tbsp zero calorie brown sugar alternative (I use Pure Via)

100ml light soy sauce

1 tbsp sesame oil

2 tbsp sriracha sauce

1 tbsp cornflour

1. First, to make the sauce, combine all the ingredients in a large bowl and mix well. Set aside.

2. Heat a wok over a medium heat, spray with oil, then add the peppers and stir-fry for 3 minutes. Remove the peppers from the pan and set aside.

3. Turn up the heat, then add the steak and sear on all sides; turn the heat down to medium and cook for a further 2 minutes.

4. Put the peppers back in the pan along with the noodles and stir-fry for a further 2 minutes.

5. Add the sauce and stir to coat all the ingredients.

6. Divide into four equal portions and add to meal prep containers. Serve sprinkled with sesame seeds.

Serves 4 | **Nutrition** | 513 calories | 40g protein | 49g carbs | 16g fat

GREEN LENTIL, CHORIZO and SMOKY BACON SOUP

As a young lad I was straight-up addicted to smoky bacon crisps. So I thought it was only right to recreate that taste sensation in a soup, bolstered with the lovely flavour of chorizo. You might call this one a marriage made in heaven, with 38 grams of protein but with the same buzz those smoky bacon crisps give you.

You could double up the quantities here to stock up your fridge or freezer, ready for lunches at work, or something for the whole family to eat together.

10–12 sprays light cooking oil

1 onion, finely chopped

2 garlic cloves, finely chopped

8 smoked bacon medallions, diced

100g chorizo, diced

2 tbsp curry powder

1 litre chicken stock

1 tbsp smoked paprika

1 tsp dried oregano

1 x 400g tin chopped tomatoes

1 carrot, peeled and diced

240g green lentils

salt and pepper

4 slices crusty bread

Low calorie switch:
sandwich thin or low calorie bread

1. Heat a pan over a medium heat and spray with cooking oil. Add the onion and garlic and cook until the onion has softened.

2. Add the bacon, chorizo and curry powder and fry until crispy.

3. Add the stock, smoked paprika, oregano, chopped tomatoes, carrot and lentils and bring to the boil, then cover the pan and simmer for 20 minutes until the lentils are tender.

4. Blitz the soup with a hand blender.

5. Ladle into bowls or meal prep containers. Serve with crusty bread.

Serves 4

Nutrition | 514 calories | 38g protein | 66g carbs | 10g fat

CHICKEN and SWEETCORN SOUP

You'll all love this recipe, and it reminds me of the first Chinese soup I ever tasted, from our local takeaway. This is nice and quick to throw together, and has the bonus of being really low in calories. You probably wouldn't expect it to pack a decent 26 grams of protein per serving, but we've got that side covered as well.

Cheeky wee slice of bread to soak up the last of the soup? Your call.

900ml boiling chicken stock

4 boneless skinless chicken thighs, about 400g total weight

3cm fresh root ginger, peeled and cut into matchsticks

3 tbsp light soy sauce

½ tsp ground white pepper

8 spring onions, finely sliced

2 x 200g tins sweetcorn, drained

2 eggs, beaten

handful of fresh coriander, chopped

1. Pour the stock into a large pan and add the chicken, ginger, soy sauce and white pepper.

2. Bring to the boil over a high heat, then cover the pan, turn the heat down to low and simmer for 15 minutes or until the chicken is cooked through.

3. Lift out the chicken and shred it, then drop it back in the pan.

4. Add the spring onions and sweetcorn, bring the soup back to the boil and allow to bubble for a few minutes.

5. Pour the beaten eggs into the soup in a thin stream, stirring continuously. Cook for a couple of minutes.

6. Ladle into bowls or meal prep containers. Serve with coriander scattered over the top.

TIP: Batch-cook this, take it to work and save yourself some pennies. Check those calories too!

Serves 4 | **Nutrition** | 272 calories | 26g protein | 13g carbs | 12g fat

GAMMON *and* PEA SOUP

Have you ever heard the phrase 'it'll warm the cockles of your heart'? That phrase was written for this soup. It's a natural choice for work lunches and a great option to have in the fridge or freezer.

Feel free to dip in some sourdough bread or seeded bread.

3 unsmoked gammon steaks
1 tbsp light unsalted butter
2 onions, finely diced
4 celery sticks, finely chopped
4 garlic cloves, finely chopped
40g plain flour
1 litre vegetable stock
800g frozen garden peas
1 tsp chilli flakes
2 tbsp light crème fraîche
handful of fresh mint, finely chopped
salt and pepper
4 slices crusty tiger bread

Low calorie switch:
sandwich thin or low calorie bread

1. Preheat the grill to medium. Grill the gammon steaks for 10–12 minutes, flipping halfway.
2. Meanwhile, in a large pan over a medium heat, melt the butter, then gently fry the onions, celery and garlic until soft.
3. Add the flour and stir well, then gradually stir in all the vegetable stock.
4. Bring to a simmer, then add the peas and cook for 2–3 minutes.
5. Remove from the heat and blitz with a hand blender until smooth.
6. Put the pan back on the heat, add the chilli flakes and season to taste with salt and pepper.
7. Chop the gammon steak and add to the soup, along with the crème fraîche and mint leaves and mix well.
8. Ladle into bowls or meal prep containers. Serve with crusty bread.

Serves 4 | **Nutrition** | 479 calories | 45g protein | 65g carbs | 10g fat

ONE TRAY, NAE STRESS

I used to think meal prep was a messy business and would use a lot of pots, pans and automobiles. Okay, maybe not that last part. But this one is the epitome of straightforward. Only one tray!

There's a bit of chopping and peeling for this but it all goes into one dish and produces four hearty portions packed with healthy veg. It delivers 51 grams of protein for just 594 calories: ideal if you're training or trying to lose weight.

Chicken thighs are a little cheaper than chicken breast, so this recipe is great if you're watching the pennies.

9 boneless skinless chicken thighs
300g sweet potatoes, peeled and chopped
60g chorizo, diced
2 red onions, cut into wedges
2 yellow peppers, roughly chopped
4 large tomatoes, roughly chopped
2 green chillies, finely chopped
2 garlic cloves, finely chopped
2 tbsp olive oil
1 tbsp paprika
1 tbsp garlic powder
1 tbsp onion salt
1 tbsp dried oregano
salt and pepper

1. Preheat the oven to 220°C/ 200°C fan/gas 7.
2. In a large ovenproof dish or baking tray, combine all the ingredients and mix well to ensure everything is coated.

3. Bake for 45 minutes until the chicken is cooked through. Divide into four equal portions and add to meal prep containers.

TIP: This is a superb option, whether you're cooking for the family or entertaining. With little involvement, you're free to run around after the kids or, even better, relax with a glass of choice.

Serves 4 | **Nutrition** | 594 calories | 51g protein | 35g carbs | 29g fat

GAMMON STEAK POTATO GRATIN

Say whaaaaat?! Yes, you read that correctly. Layers and layers of pure joy. Eat it straight away or pack in containers and reheat at work or when you get home and need a treat.

It's a creamy potato and bacon bake with a massive 48 grams of protein, perfect for anyone who is training regularly and looking to build muscle.

Using condensed soup saves you having to make a sauce from scratch. Layer it up and get stuck in.

10–12 sprays light cooking oil
3 gammon steaks, cut into large cubes
1 leek, sliced
2 garlic cloves, finely chopped
1 tin condensed mushroom soup
500g potatoes, thinly sliced
150g light Cheddar, grated
400g steamed broccoli

1. Preheat the oven to 210°C/190°C fan/gas 6½.
2. Heat a pan over a medium heat and lightly spray with cooking oil. Add the gammon and cook for 8–10 minutes until browned. Remove from the pan and set aside.
3. Spray some more oil into the pan, add the leek and garlic, cover the pan and cook for 8–10 minutes until the leek has softened.
4. Pour in the mushroom soup, mix well and heat for 2 minutes before putting the gammon steak back in.

5. Spray an ovenproof dish with cooking oil, then add a third of the potatoes.
6. Layer a third of the gammon mixture on top, followed by 50g of the cheese.
7. Repeat the potato, gammon and cheese layers twice again, finishing with cheese, then bake for 1 hour.
8. Leave to cool before adding to meal prep containers. Serve with broccoli.

 Serves 4

Nutrition | 560 calories | 48g protein | 38g carbs | 26g fat

TIP: If you don't have a steamer, pop the broccoli in a meal prep container with a splash of water, then into the microwave for 2 minutes. Easy peasy!

AUBERGINE MOUSSAKA

This one is perfect if you're trying to cut down your meat consumption while maintaining a high intake of protein. This meal delivers 31 grams of protein per serving, most of which comes from the lentils. With layer upon layer of yumminess, this packs a real punch in the taste department.

It's superb for reheating and I'm sure your friends at work will be pestering you for a wee taste. Make it vegan by sourcing some plant-based mozzarella and you're good to go.

450g aubergine
20 sprays light cooking oil
1 tbsp garlic powder
1 onion, finely diced
4 garlic cloves, finely chopped
3 tbsp tomato purée
2 tbsp zero calorie white sweetener
1 tbsp ground cinnamon
2 tbsp dried oregano
450g cooked lentils
2 x 400g tins chopped tomatoes
2 tbsp light soy sauce
2 sweet potatoes, very thinly sliced
200g light mature Cheddar, grated
salt and pepper

1. Preheat the oven to 220°C/200°C fan/gas 7.
2. Cut the aubergine into 5mm chunks, place on a chopping board, spray with half the light oil, then sprinkle with salt, pepper and garlic powder. Set to the side.
3. Heat a pan over a medium heat and spray with the remaining cooking oil. Add the onion and cook until softened.
4. Add the garlic, tomato purée, sweetener, cinnamon and 1 tablespoon of the oregano and mix well.
5. Add the lentils, tomatoes, a splash of water and soy sauce and bring to a simmer, stirring occasionally until the sauce thickens.
6. Put half the aubergine in an ovenproof dish, then spoon in a quarter of the sauce mixture. Add half the sweet potato followed by half the cheese, then more sauce.
7. Repeat the layers but this time spoon the sauce over the potato layer and scatter the cheese on top. Sprinkle with the remaining oregano.
8. Bake for 1 hour.
9. Leave to cool before slicing and adding to meal prep containers.

Serves 4 | **Nutrition** | 489 calories | 31g protein | 63g carbs | 12g fat

VEGGIE HIGH PROTEIN TIPS

Hitting your protein goals as a vegetarian or vegan is not as difficult as you might think, and there're lots of good options to pick from (even more nowadays). I've listed some of my go-tos below:

- Eggs are great and have a high satiety score. They can go in almost anything.

- Tofu is one I'll use from time-to-time. Really easy to cook, and it soaks up the surrounding flavour well; also packed with protein and contains a range of essential amino acids.

- Wholemeal bread, rice, pasta – all better than their white/plain counterparts when it comes to both protein and satiety.

- Soya chunks or flour – soya is packed with protein; in some cases, it has a higher protein content than meat per 100g. The flour can be used for your baking to add a protein boost there.

- Lentils – another great option, and so easy to use. I simply rinse mine from the can and add into a curry or pasta dish. They are superb in a dhal!

- Seitan – one of the lesser-known options here, but again packed with protein and very easy to include in a number of meals. Seitan can provide up to 75g protein per 100g!

MY GO-TO SIDES

These are some really simple side dishes that will make it that little bit easier to meet your calorie target. I use a lot of microwave sides because they're convenient and help with portion control.

Breads *and* Baked Goods 206
Rice *and* Grains 207
Noodles 208
Vegetables 209

BREAD and BAKED GOODS

Nowadays supermarkets are great at offering high protein and low calorie alternatives when it comes to baked goods. There are many brands out there – and you'll have to experiment to find your favourites. Here, as well as general guidance on portions, I've mentioned a few of the brands that I use in my recipes.

Low calorie bread
(I use Hovis Nimble Wholemeal)
1 slice = 50 calories
2.7g protein / 8g carbs / 0.6g fat

Sandwich thins
A great switch for lower calorie burgers and sandwiches
1 thin = 100 calories
5g protein / 20g carbs / 1g fat

Crusty white bread
1 slice = 103 calories
3.9g protein / 20.2g carbs / 0.5g fat

Crusty tiger bread
1 slice = 126 calories
4.7g protein / 24g carbs / 1g fat

Seeded bread
1 slice = 133 calories
4g protein / 19g carbs / 3g fat

Low calorie wrap
(I use Deli Kitchen Carb Lite)
1 wrap = 127 calories
6.9g protein / 14.6g carbs / 3.2g fat

Thin bagel
(I use Warburtons Protein Thin Bagels)
1 bagel = 160 calories
8.5g protein / 23.5g carbs / 2.8g fat

RICE and GRAINS

I use microwave rice a lot as it's quick, easy and helps with portion control. If you're looking for a cheaper option and buying larger packs of rice, follow the pack instructions for cooking times.

White rice

70g per person (dry weight)
= 241 calories (cooked)
4.7g protein / 54.4g carbs / 0g fat

Brown rice

75g per person (dry weight)
= 265 calories (cooked)
5.2g protein / 55.5g carbs / 2g fat

Long grain and wild rice

75g per person (dry weight)
= 221 calories (cooked)
4.3g protein / 45.3g carbs / 1.9g fat

Long grain microwave rice

125g per person (cooked weight)
= 170 calories
3g protein / 35g carbs / 2g fat

Basmati microwave rice

125g per person (cooked weight)
= 166 calories
3.4g protein / 34.3g carbs / 1.5g fat

Pilau basmati microwave rice

(I use Tilda)
125g per person (cooked weight)
= 161 calories
4g protein / 31g carbs / 2.3g fat

Jasmine microwave rice

125g per person (cooked weight)
= 179 calories
3.6g protein / 35.2g carbs / 2.4g fat

Wholegrain microwave rice

125g per person (cooked weight)
= 192 calories
4.9g protein / 37.8g carbs / 1.8g fat

Konjac microwave rice

(I use Better Than Rice)
125g per person (cooked weight)
= 44 calories
0.1g protein / 10.5g carbs / 0.18g fat

Packet roasted vegetable couscous

(I use Ainsley Harriott)
50g per person (dry weight)
= 177 calories (cooked)
6.3g protein / 33g carbs / 1.5g fat

NOODLES

Straight to wok rice noodles
150g per person
= 208 calories
4g protein / 45g carbs / 1g fat

Straight to wok medium noodles
150g per person
= 227 calories
8g protein / 39g carbs / 3g fat

Fine egg noodles
50g (1 nest) per person (dry weight)
 = 174 calories (cooked)
7g protein / 34g carbs / 1g fat

Medium egg noodles
145g per person (cooked weight)
= 206 calories
7g protein / 40g carbs / 1g fat

VEGETABLES

As with any healthy diet, it's important to make sure you are eating a wide range of fruit and veg. Here are a few of my favourite veg sides, including some low calorie swaps for rice and spaghetti to help you hit that five a day ideal.

Mixed leafy salad
Rocket, lettuce and spinach with 1 tbsp low calorie mustard vinaigrette
100g per person = 31 calories
1g protein / 2g carbs / 0g fat

Crunchy salad
Salad leaves, edamame beans and shredded carrot with 1 tbsp reduced fat French dressing
100g per person = 60 calories
4g protein / 6g carbs / 2g fat

Rainbow salad
Lettuce, cherry tomatoes, sliced peppers and beetroot with 1 tbsp low calorie balsamic dressing
105g per person = 50 calories
1g protein / 5g carbs / 1g fat

Cauliflower rice
You can buy this in packs, ready to microwave, in most supermarkets. It's also simple to make using fresh cauliflower: chop the cauliflower and blitz in a food processor – don't overdo it or you'll end up with a purée. Cover and cook in the microwave for about 3 minutes or until just tender.
125g per person (cooked weight) = 30 calories
2.3g protein / 2.6g carbs / 0.3g fat

Courgette spaghetti
You can buy 'courgetti' (spiralised courgettes), ready to microwave, in some supermarkets. You can make your own using a spiraliser, or by dragging the courgette down the largest holes of a box grater. Cover and cook in the microwave for about 2 minutes.
125g per person (cooked weight) = 26 calories
2.3g protein / 2.3g carbs / 0.5g fat

vegetables continued...

Mashed potatoes

Peel the potatoes, cut into chunks, then boil until soft. Drain and mash with salt and pepper and 5g light butter per person. Most supermarkets sell packs of mashed potato, ready to microwave, but check the calories as they may vary. Stick to the basic ones: luxury mash with cream and extra butter will blow your calorie budget.

150g per person = 139 calories (cooked)

2.8g protein / 23.5g carbs / 3.2g fat

Roast potatoes

Preheat the oven to 200°C/180°C fan/gas 6. Peel the potatoes, cut into chunks, then boil for about 10 minutes. Drain well and leave for a few minutes for the steam to disperse. Put the potatoes in a roasting tin and spray with light cooking oil. Roast for 40 minutes, turning half way through, until golden and crispy. If buying frozen, follow the pack instructions; calories may vary.

125g per person = 100 calories (cooked)

3.4g protein / 18g carbs / 1.2g fat

Baby potatoes

Boil for 15–20 minutes until soft.

175g per person = 125 calories (cooked)

3g protein / 26g carbs / 0g fat

Potato salad

100g new potatoes, boiled until soft, drained, chopped and mixed with 2 tbsp fat-free Greek-style yoghurt, 1 tbsp light crème fraîche, 1 tsp Dijon mustard, snipped fresh chives

1 serving = 127 calories (cooked)

5g protein / 21g carbs / 2g fat

Root vegetable mash

You can buy this in packs, ready to microwave, in most supermarkets but check the calories as they may vary.

200g per person = 154 calories (cooked)

2.8g protein / 26.1g carbs / 3.4g fat

Sweet potato mash

190g sweet potatoes, peeled, cut into chunks and boiled until soft. Drain and mash with salt, pepper and 10g light butter.

1 serving = 137 calories (cooked)

2g protein / 18g carbs / 5g fat

Oven-baked sweet potato fries

Preheat the oven to 220°C/200°C fan/gas 7. Scrub the potatoes, cut into thin chips and spread on a roasting tin. Spray with light cooking oil, sprinkle with salt and roast for 15–20 minutes, until crispy. You can also cook them in the air fryer at 200°C for about 8 minutes, turning halfway, until cooked through. If buying frozen, follow the pack instructions; calories may vary.

125g per person = 148 calories (cooked)
2g protein / 25g carbs / 4g fat

Asparagus spears

Steam for 4–6 minutes.
6 spears per person = 20 calories (cooked)
2g protein / 3g carbs / 0g fat

Broccoli

Steam for 4–6 minutes.
100g per person = 34 calories (cooked)
2.4g protein / 7.2g carbs / 0.4g fat

Edamame beans

Boil for 3 minutes.
65g per person = 125 calories (cooked)
9.2g protein / 3.4g carbs / 7.5g fat

Fine green beans

Steam for 4–6 minutes.
80g per person = 25 calories (cooked)
1.5g protein / 5.7g carbs / 0.1g fat

Medley of green veg

Green beans, runner beans and garden peas. Steam for 4–6 minutes then sprinkle with chopped fresh parsley and mint.

80g per person = 31 calories (cooked)
2.5g protein / 2.9g carbs / 0.3g fat

Mini corn on the cob

Boil for 10–12 minutes. If you're adding butter, don't forget to add this to the calorie totals.

1 mini cob = 34 calories (cooked)
2g protein / 4g carbs / 1g fat

Mushy peas

I use tinned peas then mash them with lemon and chopped fresh mint. You can also use tinned mushy peas for convenience.

100g per person = 72 calories (cooked)
4.3g protein / 11.5g carbs / 0.4g fat

Honey-glazed carrots

Part boil peeled carrots for 8 minutes, drain then drizzle with honey and cook in the air fryer at 200°C for 3–4 minutes or in a preheated oven at 220°C/200°C fan/gas 7 for about 15 minutes until crisp.

200g carrots + 1 tsp honey per person = 102 calories (cooked)
3g protein / 45g carbs / 0g fat

INDEX

ackowledgements

It's been emotional.
I know this is the part where I'm meant to thank family, friends, publishers etc and I'll get to that ... However, I feel it's only right to start with you.

I wouldn't be writing this without you. Whether you've followed me since day one or simply picked this up in a local bookshop, your support means the world to me. It sounds like a cliché, but this really doesn't happen to people like me. You made this happen and I'm forever grateful.

You might see my big head on the front cover, but a tonne of work has gone into this book from a lot of very valued people. I can't thank my fiancé, Lorrie, enough for her constant help and support; my brother, Andy, and mum, Maryan, for their input and counsel; and my wider family. I'm a very lucky guy in terms of having the right people around me.

To the team at Ebury and everyone behind the scenes, thanks for putting your faith in me. From day one the support, guidance and feedback has been invaluable, and obviously this would have never happened without you all.

BRUNCH
notes

QUICK BITES
notes

FAMILY
FAVOURITES
notes

FAKEAWAY
notes

AIR FRYER and
SLOW COOKER
notes